For The Sake Of America III

Sheila Holm

John 10:27. *My sheep hear My voice, and I know them, and they follow Me.*

Romans 8:14. *For as many as are led by the Spirit of God, these are sons of God.*

Acts 5:38. *And now I say to you, keep away from these men and let them alone; for if this plan or this work is of men, it will come to nothing 39 but if it is of God, you cannot overthrow it – lest you even be found to fight against God.*

For The Sake Of America III

For The Sake Of America III

ISBN-13: 978-1724921628
ISBN-10: 1724921622

Unless otherwise indicated all scriptures are taken from the
New King James version of the Bible.

Web Site: hisbest4us . org or sheila holm . org

Facebook: HISBest4us, Sheila Holm Christian Author

Printed in USA by HIS Best Publishing

DEDICATION

To Carol Marfori for being an editor, prayer partner and spirit filled prayer warrior willing to stand firm with me no matter what God is revealing or where God has placed my feet.

To Bishop McKinney for standing firm in prayer with me since the day we finally met in person, in 2000.

To Rebecca King who is a descendant from the tribes of Cherokee and Blackfoot, and to our Father for bringing us together and providing the depth of wisdom for the truth about the glory is: *Christ gave us the glory before He went to the cross, so we would be one as He and the Father are one.* **John 17:22.**

To Heather Rock for standing firm in truth, for remaining strong within her lineage of the Mississippians, the Muskogee Creek and Cherokee, for sharing The Apocrypha and artifacts from the Cherokee museum in Cherokee, North Carolina; photos and books which confirm the truth shared within this book, and for enjoying and sharing truth obtained during her faith walk journey!

To Rodney Howard-Browne for his willingness to share the deeper truth no matter who is in the midst of the multitude for the truth must be revealed so all believers can repent and restoration of our lives and our nation can flow like a mighty flood; for remaining strong while sharing the deeper truth within each meeting and especially in the midst of the amazing humor God provides so His message is clear and fully received.

To Bill Morford for so many reasons beyond remaining obedient until the *One New Man Bible, Revealing Jewish Roots and Power* was translated direct from the Hebrew and made available to all Christians so believers will see and know the truth: *We are no longer Gentiles, and we are not to do as the Gentiles do!* For providing the book *Fulfillment of Prophecy* by Eliezer Ben-Yehuda for our Father revealed the truth to him: *The two things without which the Jews will not be a nation: The Land and the Language.*

To all Native American Indians, with the word Indian in Hebrew being Amit and meaning an Indian is a friend, a person of Israel origin; to all who were aware of the truth, a deeper truth which was not openly revealed to the current generations.

To Tommy & Penelope Wilson for praying and knowing the truth had to be 'in a book', and to my immediate and extended family and friends for praying through and standing firm with me during these unique days in HIStory!

Table of Contents

Introduction

In the beginning GOD created ...

Wow! If we could journey back with our Father 'to the very beginning' and see His plan the way He planned it all for us from the first day forward! Wow! Trusting 'personally seeing His plan as He planned it', we would walk in faith with Him now!

He wants to show us the plan!

To align with God's plan, seek His will and desire to walk forward in faith with Him, believe 100% and command with power and authority based upon knowing His truth for He is truth!

Personally, I was going to review the first two books for you within the introduction so you could easily 'pick up this book' and be up to date in a few pages!

While I was reviewing the book, God prompted me to change everything about the introduction or the beginning. He actually changed the introduction into a chapter and moved it!

He gave me a 'surprise for you' and then, He wanted me to start in Chapter 1 the same way again exactly as song of David Phelps, *End of the Beginning*. God provides amazing surprises which confirm once again that He truly has a great sense of humor! It was a surprise but, I got a sneak peek to proceed since I trust 100%!

In my moment of trusting 100%, it still felt funny to me to merely begin without an introduction. So, the LORD immediately gave me an option.

The surprise: He reminded me of the Kendrick Brothers review of their movies in 60 seconds. It's a joy to watch! If you have not seen them, they are available on You Tube and you will be glad you took 60 seconds out of your schedule for each one!

Well, God wants me to do the same thing for you 'up front' so you can see how we progressed from *For The Sake Of America* to *For The Sake Of America II* and now, to the third book in what has become a series, *For The Sake Of America III.*

One difference you will immediately notice: A picture is worth a thousand words and there are thousands of pictures inserted into a 60 second film!

For The Sake Of America

The journey becomes personal because it includes 'over the generations' journey of Christianity, impacted by Baal/pagan worship 'without our knowledge'. Over time, it led us to this point in time in America!

Word and vision were given to the three prophets, Bob Jones, Arthur Burt and John Paul Jackson. Then, they were shared with me through their contacts, one by one. I dismissed it was 'my assignment' until I heard from the third contact who received the message from Bob Jones. He shared the details during a wedding reception near Macon.

Messages our Father shared with me, revealed during our global travel and ministry meetings across America were already released within books during the 21 days originally planned in Georgia, three weeks which turned into many months in Georgia.

Months became three years prior to the release of *For The Sake Of America.*

The LORD revealed truth through:

The Faith Monument, paid for by American Congress.

Erected 1880's; lessons to retain liberty & freedom.

Native Indians & Pilgrims provided the truth.

In a cul-de-sac directly above Plymouth Rock.

The Georgia Guidestones, the Satanic ten commandments.

Erected and dedicated in 1980.

Global plan aligned with New World Order.

Languages (8 + 4 ancient) aligned with BRICS, the new economic structure set in 2008-2010.

Macon, first Scottish Rite Temple formed by Albert Pike.

Pike (from Boston) became a General in Civil War.

Pike troop killed Native Americans; stole supplies.

Pike heard of his arrest, sent resignation letter; released from the military without trial.

Pike confirmed and declared visions from Lucifer.

Pike gathered 33rd degree Masons to proceed.

Macon, in Bibb County Georgia.

Bibb arranged illegal treaties with Native Indians.

Bibb removed Native Indians from homes & land.

Bibb sold Native land to cotton plantation owners.

Natives won in court but, homes/land already sold.

Bibb proceeded in Alabama territory as in Georgia.

Bibb appointed Alabama Governor as a thank you!

Augusta and Jekyll Island Georgia.

President Woodrow Wilson, raised in Augusta.

Federal Reserve & IRS structured on Jekyll Island.

Wilson aligned with team behind Federal Reserve.

Established a federal tax for the first time.

Wilson pushed for new constitutional amendments,

Approved immediately after inauguration:

Federal Reserve & IRS.

Senators elected by popular vote.

Wilson re-negotiated treaty with Mexico.

Wilson involved with change of Russian leadership.

Wilson structured plan for US participation, WWI.

Wilson involved in establishing League of Nations,
former structure of the United Nations.

Wilson received the Nobel Peace Prize in 1920:

Negotiation, Treaty of Versailles.

Warm Springs Georgia.

President FDR established a 'Little White House'.

FDR closed banks for four days after inauguration.

FDR proceeded with an Emergency Banking Act.

Banks were reorganized. Many were closed.
Act dissolved the government of America.

Nation bankrupt and insolvent.

America stolen from citizens by this Act.

FDR Fireside Chats established to unite all in plan.

FDR signed Executive Order 6102.

Citizens to turn in all gold above $600.

Congress enacted HJR 192.

All debts made payable to Federal Reserve.

Debt only backed by fiat notes.

FDR established social welfare system.

Social Security structured.

Money from both employers & employees.

FDR established Lend Lease Act.

Money given to Britain, Russia & China.

Money to be used for war materials.

NOTE: Japan already at war with China.

Japan outrage resulted in Pearl Harbor.

FDR credited Wilson for being his mentor!

The LORD's promise: *For The Sake Of America.*

II Chronicles 7:14.

If <u>My people</u> who are <u>called by My name</u> will <u>humble themselves,</u> and <u>pray and seek My face,</u> and <u>turn from their wicked ways</u> (REPENT), *<u>then I will hear from heaven,</u> and <u>will forgive their sin</u> <u>and heal their land</u>* (RESTORE).

NOTE: The scripture was quoted often during the election of 2016. President Trump received his copy prior to the election. He loaned the book and it was not returned to him prior to his move to DC, so his team requested a second copy prior to his inauguration.

Personal Journey: Summarized in the first chapters along with descriptions of the twelve books released during the three years in Georgia.

A trip to Macon, Georgia for three days in June 2013 resulted in a three week trip in October 2013. Only two weeks in San Diego, California since October 2013: One week in October 2015 (invitation to a Benny Hinn taping; trip turned into so much more!) before the book was written (plus, one week in October 2017 immediately after the second book was released; to arrange for

California car to be in Georgia due to an accident on July 19 when the Georgia ministry car was rear-ended in a construction zone and totaled within days).

Trusted since three weeks turned into three years, I had 'given it my all' and it was time to leave.

Then, I heard a word: *Noah was a pastor who devoted more then 100 years to building the ark without one person accepting our Father's truth! Would you be able to devote more than 100 years to delivering the truth, Jehovah's message, without one person to accept the truth?*

Yikes! Three years seemed like forever. However, I was sinking into the seat of a hard folding chair when I heard this word.

Regardless, God knew I was ready to leave Georgia at the conclusion of the first year, the second year, and again, in 2016, weeks prior to the book appearing on typed pages.

God heard me offer to leave as soon as I returned from Alabama after completing upon my commitment to preach due to an invitation extended by a Primitive Baptist pastor. His testimony and miracle healing are powerful. They are included in the book.

Unaware of a bigger plan unfolding, I diligently worked on sharing the word and vision given to the three prophets after the vision and word were given to me by their contacts. Their contacts were prompted to find me since they were not going to be able to move to Macon, Georgia. They were unable to proceed upon or become a witness to the truth they received from the prophets who knew the truth direct from God *For The Sake Of America.* The prophtets ransitioned to heaven: Bob Jones, February 2014, Arthur Burt, August 2014, and John Paul Jackson, February 2015.

Daily, I shared the vision and word with people I trusted would share the word and vision throughout Georgia so I could be released from the assignment!

God confirmed to the prophets if the people would repent, restoration would result in blessings flowing in Georgia and then, across America like a mighty flood.

God positioned two Angelic vortexes over Macon, Georgia and Moravian Falls, North Carolina, *For The Sake Of America*. God arranged for me to be in Moravian Falls and Prayer Mountain. Plus, spend a night in one of the ministry homes for rent by Morningstar ministry established by Rick Joyner.

Blessings flowed freely. Prayers were immediately answered. It was evident Rick Joyner gathered together many from the family of believers to become residents in the region. Now, to carry the truth to Macon, Georgia. Not so easy!

God started showing me, without my knowledge at the time, how the lies seeded in Georgia were shared as truth from generation to generation. He confirmed many 'seeds were sown' in Georgia to destroy America by people who did not live in Georgia!

All effort to share the facts so I could depart from Georgia resulted in Georgians telling me 'too much information to take in' and then, 'let us know when the facts are in a book so we can read and re-read the facts until we can digest them and then, maybe we can do something about them'.

What? I'm the one who is not from Georgia! I asked God for another confirmation, something current.

God provided a stack of confirmations plus a current one! News stories shared the fact that the 'team organized to stop Trump as a candidate and therefore, to stop Trump from being elected President met in Georgia'.

Yes. They actually flew to Georgia in their private jets to attend their secret meeting on Sea Island, Georgia.

Quickly, I typed the facts God shared about Georgia on the pages within a week. Then, the editors asked so many questions during the next three weeks, the book grew to 500 pages.

After much prayer, the book was finally reduced to 300 pages, including my 'journey in Georgia' with chapters dedicated to the the significance of Macon, Augusta, and "The Little White House" in Warm Springs, Georgia, the Faith Monument and the Georgia Guidestones. Deep truth which I trusted 'told the true Georgia story'. However, God had more truth to share!

For The Sake Of America II

Readers immediately requested a second book.

However, I was preparing to leave Georgia.

At that exact moment in time, my hostess for my 'last two nights in Georgia' wanted me to go with her to help decorate for a six year old's birthday party.

The party was held the very night before my early, early, early morning departure (typically the car is packed the night before so I can begin the drive by 2 AM).

Seemed simple but, I was being directed by God toward: *For The Sake Of America II*.

'As the true story goes, I met a man ...' When he asked me about my time in Georgia, my hostess said, *She wrote a book.*

The people were gathering outside for a birthday photo. The man departed with his wife but, he returned moments later to ask, *Where were you living before God sent you to Georgia?* Yikes ... I was in for a shock. When I said, *San Diego*, the man responded, *That's what God just told me.*

Then, he explained: *I was supposed to come to Georgia and the confirmation was provided* (25 years prior to my arrival in Georgia) *by a prophet involved with the Brownsville Revival. The prophet informed the leadership to gather in Albany, Georgia because the move of God was going to pour into Georgia.* The prophet returned and reminded them of the exact same message: *Remain encouraged because God is preparing someone in San Diego and you will know the person when you meet them because they will already be setting off fires throughout Georgia before your introduction.*

Wow! Tears. The same hand motion he used to tell me about setting off fires was the identical hand motion used by our Father when I was in tears, feeling responsible for 'nobody getting the message or acting upon it'. God confirmed the hand motion as setting off a hand grenade in the multitude and walking away when the message delivered as God confirmed He only wanted me to deliver the message. He said I was not responsible if or when the message was heard or acted upon. Wow!

For The Sake Of America II

Requested to see the 'flow' God confirmed to the prophets before another book would be released. Prayer on Sunday evening resulted in the truth being revealed within an hour Monday morning: Flow of oil direct from the bible.

Our Father arranged the introduction and my rental car (ministry car was rear-ended the prior week) was packed to go to the north of Georgia within ten minutes.

The 'end of the beginning' became the first chapter of the book.

In the introduction, our Father focused upon 'all created in His image'! Our Father asked again and again, *What were we thinking?*

We the People of America were busy separating, segregating the people. The Native Americans were auctioned, separated from family members, enslaved and lynched (meaning, hung without a trial); forced out of their homes and off their land by new pioneers, new settlers upon the land allowed to 'stake a claim' by the government even upon land given to the Native Americans to 're-settle or re-establish'.

Albany

Returned to Albany ... my journey includes God's humor!

Alladin's Lamp Prophecy: Din, means servant of Alla.

Moultrie

Learned the Native Americans were the first black slaves.

Learned very few came from Africa (a few 'mixed in').

Families were separated and children were fostered.

Records of family history placed in county offices.

County offices burned during Civil War; records lost.

Augusta

Returned to Augusta – Healing Springs on God's Acre.

Cherokee fought for the truth in America's Supreme Court.

Cherokee won the court case.

President Jackson knew court could not enforce.

Indian Removal Act of 1830 resulted in removal.

Christian ministers and missionaries aligned, imprisoned.

They were sent to hard labor camps.

Natives knew land belonged to God; not deeded to people.

Smallest Church in America, Memory Park near Darien.

Deeded to Jesus Christ.

Ancient Roots and History Revealed

Truth reveals Tribes of Israel traveled to America.

Ten Commandments etched in stone by Cherokee.

Stone in Paleo Hebrew from at least 5th Century BC.

Faith Monument and Georgia Guidestones

Americans Are At Choice

The truth was revealed. Trusting the information was complete and my Georgia assignment was drawing to a close.

However, God actually confirmed 'from now on' vs. 'for now'! Yikes! While I was 'in a panic – not knowing how to begin to become a Georgian', people were trying to give me a deposit for the third book in the series. Confusion seemed to surround me!

I was completely clear: *Not able to accept a deposit since there are no plans for a third book in the series.*

After hearing 'the book leads to the next book' so many times, I asked for an independent review.

During a weekend trip 'away from Georgia' arranged by a dear friend, the reviewer said the exact same thing! I was clear it did not mean a third book was going to happen, once again, because I wrote the books and they do not lead into a 'next book'.

The facts are revealed to me, layer by layer. The book is complete 'as is' each time.

It was not known to me at the time that another, deeper level story was available. However, the journey has continued in Georgia and our Father has provided significant depth of truth which is being revealed to you now, within the this book which has officially become a series: *For The Sake Of America III.*

For The Sake Of America III

> *Trumpet Call to America! Deeper Truth Revealed.*
>
> *More Repentance Required for Full Restoration.*
>
> **John 10:27.** *My sheep hear My voice, and I know them, and they follow Me.* **Romans 8:14.** *For as many as are led by the Spirit of God, these are sons of God.*

Chapter 1   Truth Revealed, Significance to America

Amazing! Our Father is absolutely amazing!

As you already know, my resistance was significant to the mere mention of one person after another after another who looked forward to reading a second book after the release of *For The Sake Of America*.

Therefore, I trust you can even visualize my facial expressions when I was approached by one person after another offering to give me a deposit for a third book in the series!

Little did I realize my challenging God process was unfolding once again. Finally, when I thought my request for our Father to confirm His plan did not include a third book, His response was quite a unique surprise. His surprise was delivered to me within the hour of my specific request!

My request was clear and specific, so I trusted it would stop the repeated offers to give me a deposit for a third book in the series: *If there is a strong scriptural reference for a third book, I will put the other books aside, again, and I will immediately proceed to format the stack of facts provided since the release of the second book: For The Sake Of America II.*

Without a moments hesitation, God prompted me to call a dear friend, a deep man of God who lives and works in the mountain region of Northeast Georgia.

Cliff Brown lives and works in Habersham County where our LORD sent me in 2015 'to gain a new, mountain top perspective'. The journey was scheduled within days of receiving the message directly from the contact of Bob Jones during a wedding reception.

God introduced me to Cliff at a prayer meeting with fellow prayer warriors during a weekly, Wednesday noon meeting of Habersham United Believers (HUB).

Personally trusting this call would be a great time of hearing the new, deep testimonies from Cliff. However, I was not prepared to hear the facts God orchestrated shortly before the call.

Cliff was reviewing an email from a woman who was also sent to the exact same mountain top location for a short period of time, about 30 days. She left the region after her short visit to Habersham & traveled back to Israel where she resides to this day.

Cliff was comparing the woman's quest for truth by saying she has a heart for the truth and God provided specific new details to her each time she asked to know the facts, exactly as Cliff observed about me when he personally witnessed how our Father worked with and through me while I was on the mountain top.

While Cliff was speaking, God was already confirming the scripture reference was being provided to me for me to proceed with and release the stacks of facts God has provided to me since the release of *For The Sake Of America II.*

My resistance was halted immediately!

Between us and to keep my slate clear, I've already repented to our Father for trusting my challenge of aligning directly with scripture would result in releasing me from proceeding with another book about Georgia! Our God proceeded exactly as He did 'within the hour' this time as He did 'within an hour the next morning' after a night of intense prayer asking for verification of the promised flow starting in Georgia before the second *For The Sake Of America* book could be released. Only God knew there was 'a steady flow of oil direct from the bible' in North Georgia, a flow which started six months before I made my request. As you know by now, God's confirmation with the flow of oil from the bible resulted in proceeding immediately with the release of *For The Sake Of America II.*

Now, *For The Sake Of America III* has become my full focus. God provided the scripture immediately and confirmed how deep the believers have become encased in a multi-layered web of deceit.

Scripture Reference Provided

Due to no internet access at the time, I tried to view the lengthy email on my phone. It was really tough!

Cliff rarely shares emails. This time, he shared a lengthy email from the woman who returned to Israel before sharing what God revealed to her.

WOW! Grateful for Cliff's clue to quickly scroll to the end since the email continued for a significant number of pages, a fact which is even more pronounced due to viewing the pages of the email on my phone!

Tears flowed as I read the words shared by Nancy Kaplan. Her ministry is Gates of Prayer. The words she shared are identical to the first two paragraphs on the website for the history of the City of Baldwin, Georgia:

The City of Baldwin, Georgia ... (established, positioned) on some 250 acres along the Banks / Habersham County line and resting on the Appalachian Continental Divide. It was originally known as Stonepile because of a large pile of stones that once stood in the center of town.

The stone structure was erected and left behind by the Cherokee Indians who once roamed these lands in abundance. The stone piling's significance to the Cherokee and why they left it remains a mystery and is now forever lost.

Remains a mystery?

Mystery to the residents to this day?

Forever lost?

LORD immediately confirmed: *Stones of Remembrance* as Holy Spirit tears (the tears that flow over the lower lids) flowed and flowed.

Stones of Remembrance

The Memorial Stones. Joshua 4:1-7.

And it came to pass, when all the people had completely crossed over the Jordan, that the Lord spoke to Joshua, saying:

2 *"Take for yourselves twelve men from the people, one man from every tribe, 3 and command them, saying, 'Take for yourselves twelve stones from here, out of the midst of the Jordan, from the place where the priests' feet stood firm. You shall carry them over with you and leave them in the lodging place where you lodge tonight.'"*

4 Then Joshua called the twelve men whom he had appointed from the children of Israel, one man from every tribe; 5 and Joshua said to them: *"Cross over before the ark of the Lord your God into the midst of the Jordan, and each one of you take up a stone on his shoulder, according to the number of the tribes of the children of Israel, 6 that this may be a sign among you when your children ask in time to come, saying, 'What do these stones mean to you?' 7 Then you shall answer them that the waters of the Jordan were cut off before the ark of the covenant of the Lord; when it crossed over the Jordan, the waters of the Jordan*

were cut off. And these stones shall be for a memorial to the children of Israel forever."

Train Up A Child In The Way They Will Go

We are wondering what has happened in the current generation while <u>the truth is: changes in the education process have drastically changed how the next generation hears facts, especially if the facts shared are actually lies repeated generation to generation.</u>

To retain our freedom and liberty, we need to train up Christians to hear the voice of the Father vs. the voices in the world regarding how to live our lives.

We must only proceed based upon knowing and hearing the voice of GOD. This has not been our Christian focus across America for the past two hundred years. We changed from families training up the children in the way they should go to giving the education process over to the government.

What happened? Families wanted each of the next generations to 'do more, better' than the current generation so the families sacrificed physically and financially to provide more education for each of their children by the government. Then, the next generations were supported in 'competing to be better than prior generations'. Competition is evident in families, between siblings & spouses. The impact upon the family and community is obvious.

Generations over time have learned 'a version of the truth' while the truth is 'there are no versions of the truth'.

There is only the truth within the truth! No leaven in truth!

Lies (leaven) have been repeated as facts but, the facts being repeated were never the true facts, the truth.

We were taught how to become successful 'in the world' vs. listening to God's voice to hear the truth direct from our Father!

Over time, the education process has become 'repeating the lies' until the truth appears to be 'forever lost'!

The people who fought for the truth on behalf of the Native people, the Native Indians, were imprisoned and forced into labor camps. They were missionaries and ministers who knew the truth and they were fighting for the truth to be revealed about the Native Indians so they would not be removed based upon a newly structured Native Indian Removal Act. The missionaries knew the truth about 'who Native Indians were'. The Pilgrims knew. Jews on the ships who sailed with Columbus knew. Each of these groups blended together with the Native Indians in truth for more than 200 and 300 years before a few in the government chose to change the rules for the people who resided free on the land for more then 2300 years! *LORD forgive us!*

Most of the tens of thousands of Native Indians living in unsettled land across America had no idea that a Native Indian Removal Act existed or that the quick decision of a few on the East coast of the land would change their lives forever!

GOD forgive us! We have so much we need to repent for, whether we took the actions or not, due to continuing to repeat the lies as truth which continues the curse upon our land to this day!

GOD reminded me this morning of the statement I was repeating constantly since the age of four (experience explained at length in my book: *It's A Faith Walk!,* God has confirmed many times when the next assignment seems too big, since He asked me, *Don't you want to do what I want you to do?* To which I quickly replied, *I will do anything You want me to do.).*

The statement which I was stating again and again in the the meadow of our family farm is a statement which remains true to this day: *They are really nice people but, they just don't get it!*

People were going to church every Sunday but, daily life did not reflect God's plan between the Sunday gatherings.

Constantly during the next five years (age 4-9) I was told to stop giving messages to the people. Since the need was significant and because the people were not hearing our Father's voice even when He was shouting the messages, I continued.

Due to family requests, I stopped when I was nine. The timing is easy to remember since both of my grandfathers transitioned to heaven when I was eight. They always wanted to know what I was hearing and I was intrigued by their stories about what they knew due to my mother's father being from Scottish heritage and my father's father actually immigrating through Ellis Island from Norway. Their accents were exciting to listen to while they told me what their lives were like when they were young.

Back to our Father's plan for me. Now, I realize why our LORD often prompts me to tell people in the prayer lines: *May you hear the voice of our Father even when He whispers.*

People thought it was not credible for me to think our Father was talking to me at the age of four. I took their concern to our LORD and I've been receiving direct confirmations from a four year old in each location where God has placed my feet globally and now, across America and even in Georgia.

GOD makes it clear to us. We just forget. GOD sends the children. GOD's children hear their Father's voice.

Now, He is confirming the current status in America is exactly why He prompted me to realize 'they do not get it' so it is all making sense with what is finally being revealed across America. It is also making sense why GOD chose to send me to Georgia for these exact days in our American HIStory. God knew I would do what He wanted me to do, say what He wanted me to say so His purpose and plan can be fulfilled upon in these days.

This being said, it's not about me! GOD loves us so much that He sent His son that each of us might know His truth and learn how to hear His voice to do and say what He wants us to do and say in these days.

In fact, this October will be five years since the day our Father placed my feet in Georgia. He has positioned me in nearly every region of Georgia 'on purpose'. He knew the plan. He knew I would do all I could to complete the assignment and 'move on'.

It is clear that church attending and volunteering is doing well throughout the regions while the seeking of GOD's voice, to know that we know His purpose and plan for these days, for His destiny for each of us to become the focus is not evident.

To know what to repent for so restoration can take place is to know how to hear GOD's voice so we will each hear the truth direct from our Father, repent as directed and be restored.

We have a responsibility. We are here for His purpose and plan to be fulfilled. We have allowed many layers of lies to be repeated. Now, we need to repent for all of it because we have taken the lies on as truth and repeated the lies as though they are truth.

We either serve Baal (gods) or we serve the only living LORD.

Today, God is confirming to me as I share the truth with you that I knew a deeper truth which has taken a few decades for me to relate to, repent for and be restored. Example: Doing everything I was told to do while obtaining levels of education. Over time, becoming a repeater of what even the religion and philosophy professors wanted to hear me state. Not all truth. The lies in the many classes, even in Christian universities, required me to meet their goal: *To be successful in the world, get good grades!*

My success was amazing. It seemed to have advantages but, it resulted in the world doing everything to compete with me and to stop me, before I knew I was more valuable to the LORD!

Now, GOD is revealing that all of the experiences GOD has walked through with me have led me to this exact point in time.

These days are a critical time in our history on earth, a time when I can finally see the many layers impacting us, our lives, as the 'legal citizens on the land'.

History is getting ready to repeat a devastating blow to the 'Americans living on the land' if we do not wake up, repent and pray for restoration of our land, our personal 'hunk of dust' and the land of our blessed nation!

II Chronicles 7:14. *If <u>My people</u> who are <u>called by My name</u> will <u>humble themselves</u>, and <u>pray and seek My face</u>, and <u>turn from their wicked ways</u>* (REPENT), *<u>then I will hear from heaven</u>, and <u>will forgive their sin</u> <u>and heal their land</u>* (RESTORE).

What is the meaning of a stone in Hebrew?

A stone means a rock and so much more!

GOD is enjoying the process of sending me to the Hebrew meanings for each key word!

So, I asked God for a good scripture for stone and He directed me to a specific scripture:

Zechariah 3:9-10.

> For behold, the stone
> That I have laid before Joshua:
> Upon the stone *are* seven eyes.
> Behold, I will engrave its inscription,'
> Says the Lord of hosts,
> 'And I will remove the iniquity of that land in one day.
> **10** In that day,' says the Lord of hosts,
> 'Everyone will invite his neighbor
> Under his vine and under his fig tree.' "

A big message about who we are to be with the stone being the truth and the word, Christ! I was still contemplating the depth of the message when GOD prompted me to review verses **prior to Zechariah 3:9.**

Zechariah 3. Vision of the High Priest

Then he showed me Joshua the high priest standing before the Angel of the LORD, and Satan standing at his right hand to oppose him. 2 And the LORD said to Satan, *"The LORD rebuke you, Satan! The LORD who has chosen Jerusalem rebuke you! Is this not a brand plucked from the fire?"*

3 Now Joshua was clothed with filthy garments, and was standing before the Angel.

4 Then He answered and spoke to those who stood before Him, saying, *"Take away the filthy garments from him."* And to him He said, *"See, I have removed your iniquity from you, and I will clothe you with rich robes."*

5 And I said, *"Let them put a clean turban on his head."*

So they put a clean turban on his head, and they put the clothes on him. And the Angel of the LORD stood by.

The Coming Branch

6 Then the Angel of the LORD admonished Joshua, saying,

7 *"Thus says the LORD of hosts:*

'If you will walk in My ways,
And if you will keep My command,
Then you shall also judge My house,
And likewise have charge of My courts;
I will give you places to walk
Among these who stand here.

8 'Hear, O Joshua, the high priest,
You and your companions who sit before you,
For they are a wondrous sign;
For behold, I am bringing forth
My Servant the BRANCH.

Then, **Zechariah 3:9.**

9 For behold, the stone
That I have laid before Joshua:
Upon the stone are seven eyes.
Behold, I will engrave its inscription,'
Says the LORD of hosts,
'And I will remove the iniquity of that land in one day.
10 In that day,' says the LORD of hosts,
'Everyone will invite his neighbor
Under his vine and under his fig tree.' "

May the message bless you as much as it has blessed me for we have a lot of repenting to do before we are truly united together in truth, to represent 'A Peculiar People, A Holy Nation', a true family of GOD, people our Father will call *MY PEOPLE, a people who are called by MY NAME!*

Will We Seek Truth And Operate In Truth?

Will We Repent For The Lies?
Or, Will We Continue To Repeat Lies As Truth?
Our America, Our Future is at Stake!

Praying we will repent for the repeated lies and the actions taken against the people sharing the truth, and seek restoration of our land, beginning with our life since we are each the unique 'hunk of dust' our LORD formed 'in His image' and sent to Earth for these unique days in HIStory to fulfill upon our destiny, also known as His purpose and plan for us in these days!

LORD help us! Help us to seek Your truth!

Help us to clearly hear Your voice and help others so they will learn how to hear Your voice! Help us to hear Your voice even when You whisper.

Help us seek your truth about everything on a daily basis.

Help us sharpen each other as iron sharpens iron so we will be ready when the moment arrives to be Your representative!

Help us to pull away from the world and align with Your will!

Help us hear what we need to repent for whether we took the actions against Your people or not!

Help us to know Your truth so we will know who we are as Your people, who we are grafted in with as Your family, so we will align with them to fulfill upon Your purpose and plan for these days!

In the mighty and matchless name of our LORD and Savior Jesus Christ, our Yeshua Hamashiach we pray.

AMEN (our God is a faithful King)

Chapter 2   To All Believers, The Significance of Stones

Significance of a Stone, Eben: Hebrew meaning.

<u>Eben</u> is the word for stone or rock in Hebrew.

א ב ן

God the Father

Aleph, א is the first character in the Hebrew alphabet and represents God or Heavenly Father (masculine in Hebrew).

God the Son

Bet, ב combined with the Nun means Son in Hebrew or Jesus Christ (masculine in Hebrew).

God the Holy Spirit

Noun, feminine root: ‫א - ב – ן‬ Holy Spirit (feminine in Hebrew).

This time, I immediately honored the request of our Father to seek the true meaning of the word stone in Hebrew.

When our Father prompts me to research a word, I truly want to be 100% obedient. However, I resisted His request to seek the Hebrew meaning of the word Indian when God made the request within days of the release of *For The Sake Of America II*.

The meaning of the word in Hebrew is something which God wanted me to add to the book but, I resisted. Why? I leaned upon my own understanding. I trusted man's definition that Indian is a name the settlers added to the name of the Native Americans.

Clearly, I was wrong!

The truth dispels the lies, the facts shared with us as though they were the truth and 'nothing but the truth'. Lies shared as truth have created many misunderstandings. Then, the lies and misunderstandings were passed on generation to generation.

Over time, lies 'appeared to be the truth' because lies were stated by people we trusted. This is how lies have become accepted as truth for us, confirmed each time we share what the prior generations told us because they 'understood the facts' shared as truth because they trusted the person sharing the facts.

All of this happened without anyone questioning or researching the facts to be sure only the truth was being shared.

Many of the lies are dispelled within the each chapter of this book. In fact, some of the liars are identified. This is being done to help us connect the dots with the agenda of the liars, an agenda we accepted as truth but, it is an agenda operating against the people of GOD whether inside or outside of the church.

Connecting the dots helps us gain understanding as believers of the only living LORD so we will pray, seek the truth of our Father and hear His voice to begin to comprehend how far off track we are from what GOD planned for us as His people, called by His name!

The Indian word in Hebrew is provided in Chapter 4, Native Indian History, Significance to America. Due to the lies being accepted as truth, we accepted lies perpetuated within stories, TV programs and films which focus upon life of the pioneers or settlers and Native American Indians. *LORD forgive us!*

Yikes! The Native Americans lived 'free on the land granted by the Creator'. They knew 'no land belonged to individual people'. They were repeatedly forced out of their homes and pushed off their land by the government so the land could be sold and documented as 'owned by individuals'. This was NOT God's plan for the uninhabited land He gave to the tribes. Each time the Native American Indians were pushed further West, a land rush resulted in the loss of their homes and land again and again!

The reason they left the stones 'in a pile' when they departed from the land GOD gave them should not be a mystery to anyone operating in the truth. The stones had significant meaning to the Native American people and they should be revered by us, also.

In David's 24th Psalm. **The King of Glory and His Kingdom.**

The earth is the LORD's and all its fullness,

The world and those who dwell therein.

2 For He has founded it upon the seas,

And established it upon the waters.

3 Who may ascend into the hill of the LORD?

Or who may stand in His holy place?

4 He who has clean hands and a pure heart,

Who has not lifted up his soul to an idol,

Nor sworn deceitfully.

5 He shall receive blessing from the LORD,

And righteousness from the God of his salvation.

6 This is Jacob, the generation of those who seek Him,

Who seek Your face. *Selah*

LORD forgive us!

We are grafted into the tribes. We are no longer Gentiles!

We are His people! We are the generations seeking Him!

7 Lift up your heads, O you gates!

And be lifted up, you everlasting doors!

And the King of glory shall come in.

8 Who is the King of glory?

The LORD strong and mighty,

The LORD mighty in battle.

9 Lift up your heads, O you gates!

Lift up, you everlasting doors!

And the King of glory shall come in.

10 Who is the King of glory?

The LORD of hosts,

He is the King of glory. *Selah*

God assured us of His help, as the tribes, Israelites.

We want to be recognized as His people so He will not declare that He never knew us!

To be sure, what is required of us?

To be sure we are His, to have a solid foundation.

What is the solid foundation for believers?

The stone we are founded upon, our LORD, our Christ.

Psalm 118:21-23 (emphasis, underlining added).

²¹ I will praise You,

For You have answered me,

And have become my salvation.

²² The stone *which* the builders rejected

Has become the chief cornerstone.

²³ This was the LORD's doing;

It *is* marvelous in our eyes.

Isaiah 28:15-17 +.

¹⁵ Because you have said,

"We have made a covenant with death,

And with Sheol (Hades) we are in agreement.

When the overflowing scourge passes through,

It will not come to us,

For we have made lies our refuge,

And under falsehood we have hidden ourselves."

This is the reason why I explained how the lies have 'appeared to be truth' and by sharing the lies and accepting the lies as our truth actually aligns us with the enemy. The lies are what separates us from our LORD, our Christ.

40

A Cornerstone in Zion

16 Therefore, thus says the Lord GOD:

"Behold, I lay in Zion a stone for a foundation,

A tried stone, a precious cornerstone, a sure foundation;

<u>*Whoever believes will not act hastily.*</u>

17 *Also I will make justice the measuring line,*

And righteousness the plummet;

The hail will sweep away the refuge of lies,

And the waters will overflow the hiding place.

We must be careful! We can easily 'separate ourselves from the stone' so much, we question why we are not seeing justice being served upon the people in these days, the ones who operate in fraud and deceit. Over time, separation will cause the people to become a people who look to the government to bring forth justice.

Caution: Separation of church and state was included in our founding documents to keep us free and not ruled by the President deciding which church would become the Church of America.

The Founding Fathers experienced being in a church controlled by the government. They had to attend and align with 'man's church' by order of the King for both the Church of England and the Church of Scotland. They did not want that structure to become the future for believers within America. However, we allowed the politically correct to separate us from the truth by having all in the

41

church depart from the government. This is what kept believers from participating in the government. Instead, we were to fully participate and keep the structure of the laws and the government aligned with the structure established by the LORD.

Truth: Half of the signers of the Declaration of Independence were seminary graduates. Congress paid for the printing and distribution of the first 10,000 bibles for every church, school and home in America. Ten Commandments appeared within the Courthouses across the nation. We have allowed the removal of the Ten Commandments during the current generation!

LORD we repent!

We desire to remain close to the Chief Cornerstone.

We know our foundation is strong in Him.

We are grateful for His protection and for our salvation.

Isaiah 28:18-19.

> **18** *Your covenant with death will be annulled,*
>
> *And your agreement with Shoel (Hades) will not stand,*
>
> *When the overflowing scourge passes through,*
>
> *Then you will be trampled by it.*
>
> **19** *As often as it goes out it will take you;*
>
> *For morning by morning it will pass over,*

And by day and by night;

It will be a terror just to understand the report."

LORD we repent. Forgive us for aligning with lies, with human understanding whether known or unknown to us as lies in these days.

We desire to hear Your voice, even when you whisper. Thank you for keeping Your hand upon us and for keeping us awake and aware of Your voice for the enemy is the closest counterfeit and we will remain diligent in confirming the assignments for us in these days are based upon Your truth and Your purpose and plan for our life! AMEN

Zechariah 10:3-5.

³ *"My anger is kindled against the shepherds,*

And I will punish the goatherds.

For <u>the LORD of hosts will visit His flock,</u>

<u>The house of Judah</u> (the two tribes from the South of Israel),

<u>And will make them as His royal horse in the battle.</u>

⁴ *<u>From him comes the cornerstone,</u>*

From him the tent peg,

From him the battle bow,

From him every ruler together.

5 They shall be like mighty men,

Who tread down their enemies

In the mire of the streets in the battle.

<u>*They shall fight because the LORD is with them,*</u>

<u>*And the riders on horses shall be put to shame.*</u>

Matthew 21:41-43.

41 They said to Him, *"He will destroy those wicked men miserably, and lease his vineyard to other vine dressers who will render to him the fruits in their seasons."*

42 Jesus said to them,

> *"Have you never read in the Scriptures:*
> *'The stone which the builders rejected*
> *Has become the chief cornerstone,*
> *This was the LORD's doing,*
> *And it is marvelous in our eyes'?*
> 43 *"Therefore I say to you, the kingdom of God*
> *will be taken from you and given to a nation*
> *bearing the fruits of it.*

The message to us about rejecting the cornerstone is found again in **Mark 11:9-11, Luke 20:16-18 and Acts 4:10-12.**

Then, **Ephesians 2:18-20** identifies the structure of the gathering of believers coming together as the church.

Ephesians 2:18-20.

For through Him we both have access by one Spirit to the Father.

Christ Our Cornerstone

19 Now, therefore, you are no longer strangers and foreigners, but <u>fellow citizens with the saints and members of the household of God,</u> 20 <u>having been built on the foundation of the apostles and prophets, Jesus Christ Himself being the chief corner*stone*,</u>

For us, our life is as a stone with the Chief Cornerstone:

1 Peter 2:5-7. you also, <u>as living stones</u>, are being built up a spiritual house, a holy priesthood, to offer up spiritual sacrifices acceptable to God through Jesus Christ. 6 Therefore it is also contained in the Scripture,

> *"Behold, I lay in Zion*
> *<u>A chief cornerstone</u>, elect, precious,*
> *<u>And he who believes on Him</u>*
> *<u>will by no means be put to shame.</u>"*

^{7} <u>Therefore, to you who believe,</u> *He is* <u>precious; but to those</u> <u>who are disobedient,</u>

> *"The stone which the builders rejected*
> *Has become the chief cornerstone,"*

Great reminder to OBEY!

In fact, **I Peter 2:6-8** includes and therefore, it confirms this truth at the conclusion of the exact same warning stated above:

^{8} and

> *"A stone of stumbling*
> *And a rock of offense."*

They stumble, being disobedient to the word, to which they also were appointed.

LORD I repent!

Daily, I desire to live within Your will, listening to Your voice so closely I know it is Your voice even when you whisper for I truly want my life to be a living testimony, a stone of remembrance for all who have ears to hear your truth.

LORD I only want to say what You would have me say and do what You would have me do for I desire to be 100% obedient to Your spirit, to be recognized as a joint heir, a son of GOD!

Chapter 3 Counterfeit Stones, Significance to America

A **_huge lie_** hidden from citizens:

Research articles are based upon 'fake news', lies regarding the story about the **Georgia Guidestones in Elberton, Georgia.**

After a brief visit with my mother, sister and brother in Nebraska for Mother's Day, I was ready to hear what our LORD wanted to reveal so this book would become the completion of the series!

No cell range for nearly all of the time in Nebraska. In fact, as soon as my car continued north at Kansas City, I was without cell phone options for nearly five hours!

During my last day in Nebraska, I received an email from **Praying Medic**. He is a brand new contact. If you have not seen his blog or joined his email newsletter list, I highly recommend checking it out since it provides information you will not receive from other 'news sources'. It was Memorial Day and his TV interview with Sid Roth started airing on the same day.

Early the next morning, I began my journey southeast. Again, no cell range during my return trip to Georgia until I turned east at Kansas City.

Within seconds, I received a call from the woman who coordinates the intercessors for Mark Taylor, *Trump Prophecies*.

As soon as I answered the phone, she confirmed Mark Taylor was on the line.

Exciting for more reasons than the timing of the call since I did not have cell phone coverage moments before. Mark's movie will be released soon and I trusted he was going to talk about the two books in the series which I have shared with him due to a conversation with Mark since he was at the same Christian TV Studio in Augusta during the summer of 2017, Channel 49.

For The Sake Of America was given to Mark while he was at the studio. As soon as he held the book, he said he was going to have his intercessors pray for me and for the information being released in these days. *For The Sake Of America II* was mailed to Mark in the fall of 2017, as soon as the book was released.

In January, Mark's head of the team of intercessors called. She confirmed they were praying about the Georgia Guidestones since Mark received my book.

Mark immediately confirmed the call is due to the fact Mark received two inquiries about the Georgia Guidestones from GOD during prayer the night before:

1. Deed.

As soon as I heard the word deed, I asked if Mark thought it was *a property deed or a dirty deed hidden underground* since there is a large concrete slab immediately to the left or west side of the Guidestones.

2. Underground.

Mark asked what was underground so, I told him about *the time capsule which was placed under the concrete slab.*

GOD is revealing so much to Mark, I was deeply honored to receive the inquiries. Then, GOD prompted me to ask Mark about **Praying Medic.** Since I was brand new to Praying Medic, I thought the request was odd but, it was part of GOD's plan since Mark knows him very well.

As soon as we concluded the call, I started the research by placing calls to key sources.

Truth our Father is revealing in these days is deep!

LIES stated as truth, also accepted as truth over time:

Remember hearing it was a mystery? Lie!

Arranged by a mysterious man. Lie!

Local men involved were unaware of any facts. Lie!

Who holds the deed to the land?

The deed states the land was **given as 'a gift' to the Elbert County Board of Commissioners**.

50

Therefore, the taxpayers in Elbert County own the land. Residents are paying the budget for the Commissioners. Within the budget expenses, taxpayers are directly responsible for paying for the maintenance of the Georgia Guidestones.

The owner who gifted the land is not easily identified on the deed document per the law firm which researched the deed recorded on the property in 1979.

What was the deal on the land?

A $5,000 payment is identified as the 'gift' amount for the five acres of what still appears to be a cow pasture. It is grazing land made available for the use by the Mullinex family and their sons. Land is located on the highest hill in Elbert County Georgia.

NOTE: Department of Agriculture report states land value for agricultural land in 1979 was $679/acre. The purchase (not named or clearly identified) or 'gift' of the five acres of pasture land in Elberton, Georgia was therefore valued at $1,000/acre.

What is underground?

The research is so entangled in the scheme arranged by the exact men named, the men involved 'in the deal' that I know that I know it is best to give the facts layer by layer. Why? Truth is a complete shock. GOD is revealing 'what is hidden from view'.

Who was involved in the building of the Georgia Guidestones deal?

The three key men involved in the deal were:

1. Joe Fendley, the owner of the Granite Company, was approached by a well dressed, silver haired man who said he represented *'a small group of loyal Americans'*. Fendley was advised the stones had to survive the apocalypse and they would serve as a compass, calendar and clock,

2. Wyatt Martin, the President of the local bank who handled the transaction for a man he stated presented with an elegant appearance, confirming in the initial meeting that R C Christian was a pseudonym and he wanted to remain anonymous because he is well known, and

3. Wayne Mullinex, the owner of the land (cow pasture) where the Georgia Guidestones are located; lifetime grazing rights passed on to the son(s).

How could a deal of this magnitude be arranged while few people in Elbert County or in the State of Georgia know anything about the Georgia Guidestones?

The three men involved in the deal were actually long time residents of Elberton, Georgia. They were also members of Elberton's Masonic Lodge Philomathea # 25.

Plus, the owner of the granite company actually stated the original order for the Georgia Guidestones was considered to be a prank by one of his Shriner friends. Therefore, the three men may have also been members of the Shriners. Membership in the

Shriners is only available after Masons have completed oaths for all of the 33 degrees.

Status: **The three men directly involved in Elberton have passed away.**

Location? The Guidestones are positioned on the highest hill in the region, in a cow pasture. Grazing rights are protected for the Mullinex family with the deal stating the family can continue to use of the land for grazing.

The site is located about nine miles from the center of the town of Elberton, a short distance East of the Hartwell Highway. However, the location is not easily visible from the Hartwell Highway so only residents who would turn left and continue on the country road would know the exact location of the Georgia Guidestones.

TRUTH:

Many in the region do not know the Guidestones exist.

Many people in Georgia are unaware of the Guidestones.

Were the funds private? Perhaps.

Supposedly, the cost was paid anonymously with private funds.

A check or checks received from R. C. Christian written on checks from various banks across the country.

Supposedly, the R C Christian name was a pseudonym while the word pseudonym is misspelled on the concrete slab to the left or West side of the Guidestones. The slab allegedly covers a **time capsule** inserted prior to the revealing of the Guidestones in 1980.

Did R C Christian use a pseudonym?

Did a man named R C Christian actually exist?

Was anything known about the man who supposedly operated as an anonymous source arranging for the establishment of the Georgia Guidestones?

The man who said he was R C Christian, stated two key facts:

1. RC said he was a Christian,

2. RC said his great-grandmother was a Georgian.

Therefore, RC wanted the Guidestones to be in Georgia.

Truth: Statements on the Georgia Guidestones are not Christian. Statements are aligned with the One World Order.

Letters were provided.

People who knew the truth did not feel they could release the facts and evidence until they were close to death.

The letters confirm a well known Georgia man.

There is another person directly involved with the well known businessman, a man with the initials R C C. The research and facts obtained from the letters are being revealed, finally.

The 'behind the scenes of the deal details' are being revealed because the 'agenda against America' with the placement of the Georgia Guidestones in 1980 was a confirmation of a 100 year strategic plan which has unfolded, without detection!

We have been asleep! Layer by layer, we have been encased in a web of deceit exactly in the same fashion as placing a frog in a pot of warm water and slowly turning up the temperature until the frog is 'cooked' without realizing anything was 'terribly wrong'.

Feeling a bit cooked within the current status of America?

These are the days, so I am doing everything I can to share specifics as GOD has revealed them so we can walk through the layers of lies about America and the Guidestones.

One thing is clear, confusion was established around every fact to 'hide it' from Americans. Therefore, once again the repeated lies have been accepted as the truth. *LORD forgive us!*

How were the specific messages and Georgia selected?

The supposedly anonymous man using the pseudonym R C Christian said he was a **Christian** and his **great-grandmother was a Georgian** which is the reason why he chose Georgia as the location for the Guidestones.

1. Christian message? The **stones are not a Christian message.** The message is aligned with the One World Order which is exactly the plans described and disbursed in school textbooks by Alice and Foster Bailey through Lucis Trust Publishing (formerly Lucifer Publishing).

2. Who is the Georgian grandmother? A lot of prayer before God prompted me to research the family history for the potential of a Georgia connection.

God prompted me to research the information in **two completely different directions** to reveal truth which was clearly not known to me when I visited and researched the Guidestones for the prior books:

Dr. David R. Reagan Confirmed Lucis Trust
Headquartered within United Nations Building
United Nations Plaza in New York
The New Age Movement

Dr. David Reagan research: According to the rumor, the monument had been paid for by a mysterious group affiliated with the New Age Movement, an international amalgamation of *Humanist societies* whose aim is to prepare the way for the coming of 'Lord Maitreya', a Messiah who will save the world.

The guiding force behind the movement is the Lucis Trust located at the United Nations Plaza in New York.

Reagan confirmed the movement has been well documented in Constance Cumby's book *The Hidden Dangers of the Rainbow.*

Guidestones Message:

Let these be Guidestones to an Age of Reason is carved into the four sides of the capstone in four ancient languages:

1.   Classical Greek (dialect of less than 5,000 people located along the Black Sea),

2.   Sanskrit (India),

3.   Babylonian (sun god worshipers) and

4.   Egyptian Hieroglyphs (sun god worship; found in caves in America, even in Oklahoma, dating back more than 3500 years).

What are the languages, eight current and four ancient which exactly match the BRICS format not realized until 2010, exactly 30 years after the Guidestones were revealed in 1980.

How were the specific languages translated?

It was revealed in the past few months that the Georgia Guidestone languages were actually translated by personnel at the United Nations.

FIRST: What do we know? The United Nations housed Lucifer Publishing which was renamed Lucis Trust. Plus, a new addition or renaming of the same organization is Lifebridge Foundation. Plus, World Global Servers is an addition to the original structure as the humanitarian foundation division of Lucis Trust. All of the structures are housed within the United Nations building. American taxpayers have always paid the costs for the bulding, the maintenance of the building, and since 2000, for the extremely expensive remodel arranged & approved by Congress and paid for with American tax dollars.

New Information: Name change to Lucis Trust in about 1922 took place after Alice (divorced from Walter Evans) married Foster Bailey in 1921. They founded the new structure together while it is not actually a new entity since the Trust merely continued upon the same plan as Lucifer Publishing to print the majority (nearly all) of the public school text books.

Facts: Alice Bailey was mentored by Madame Helena Petrovna Blavatsky.

God prompted me to research her birth information: Madame Blavatsky was born (nee Princess Hahn in 1831) in Ekaterinoslav, **Georgia**. This Georgia is actually in the <u>Southern part of Russia</u> (her birth town is currently located within the Ukraine).

Who is she?

Madame Blavatsky founded the Theosophical Society.

Soldiers returning from WWI were given free memberships in the Theosophical Society.

Alice and Foster Bailey were members of the Theosophical Society in 1917, before they were married in 1921.

The Society is directly connected with New Age, New or One World Order and the Eugenics Society.

What is Eugenics, the basis of the Eugenics Society?

Since Eugenics was a new term to me, I checked the definition: *Eugenics is the science of improving a human population by controlled breeding to increase the occurrence of desirable heritable characteristics.*

How is the Time Capsule linked to Eugenics and Messages translated into eight languages upon the Georgia Guidestones?

Upon the date the Guidestones were founded supposedly by 'a group of loyal Americans' the next step will be a date they select, a date upon which they plan to reduce the population by culling.

Time capsule alleges that the date on the time capsule is not provided because it will only be inserted the day before the 'culling' of the population to reduce to 500,000,000 takes place.

Definition of cull: *To reduce a population by selective slaughter, to send inferior or surplus to be slaughtered.*

Was R C Christian a great-grandson of Madame Blavatsky?

Hours have been spent reading the pages and pages, and more pages and pages of her extensive and illustrious biography. It is clear that she did not have any children. So, R C Christian would not be her great-grandson.

Who would represent the great-grandmother?

Since the Georgia Guidestones were specifically erected in 1980, it appears it was done to honor the mentor, a Georgian, Madame Blavatsky and her trainee, Alice Bailey.

Alice Evans Bailey was born in June 1880.

So, it became the 'next phase of my research' to find out if Alice had a great-grandson who might have honored her with the Georgia Guidestones when she would have been 100 years old.

Alice Evans raised three children, daughters. Walter Evans was their father. The girls used both names, Evans with Bailey as their last name. Biography option does not include the names or details regarding her three children or that she married Foster Bailey to gain the last name. She became famous as the founder of Lucifer

59

Publishing while she was still Alice Evans but, she is recognized as a Theosophical Society leader and an author of books while records only show her as Alice Bailey. In fact, she was at the American headquarters of the Theosophical Society in Los Angeles when she met Foster Bailey. They married in Manhattan in 1921 and they lived in New York during most of their time together.

Alice and Foster were both members of the American Theosophical Society since 1917. They met while Foster was serving as the National Secretary of the American Theosophical Society in Los Angeles. Foster Bailey was born in Massachusetts. He became a 33rd degree Mason after his initiation in 1913.

They lived in New York, Connecticut and New Jersey after they arranged together to restructure Lucifer Publishing to Lucis Trust in 1922. They were not born or raised in Georgia and they did not live in Georgia during their lifetime.

Madame Blavatsky is the only connection with Georgia.

So, did Alice Bailey have a grandson who would consider Madame Blavatsky to be a great-grandmother?

God continued to prompt me to research the family of Alice (Evans) Bailey.

No clues in the biography for Alice. Only listing: 3 children.

Foster Bailey's biography, however, includes the fact Alice had three daughters while she was married to Walter Evans. Walter is the only spouse identified within the biography for Alice. Foster's biography supplied the names of Alice and her three daughters:

Dorothy, Mildred, and Ellison.

Dorothy, born in 1908 and Mildred, born in 1912 did not marry or have children.

Ellison was born in California in 1914. She married Arthur Gordon Poynter Leahy from London. They had one son Arthur Ronald William Leahy who was born in Pakistan in 1944.

Not appearing as RC Christian, a man described within the blogs, articles and letters as an elegant, silver haired man who was middle-aged in 1979.

Also, Ellison and her husband were married in Sussex, England. Ellison, her husband and their son all died and are buried in Chichester, West Sussex, England.

LORD I am still hitting a major brick wall!

Did the man who said he was R C Christian lie about a Georgia connection?

SECOND: GOD immediately confirmed the truth is available and it does include the link to Georgia for the site of the Guidestones.

GOD also confirmed there is a direct link to the 'agenda against America' Alice Bailey was focused upon, an agenda which has been unfolding 'successfully and effectively, without a change' for 100 years.

Repented, again!

Structure established by Alice Bailey is still the 100 year plan 'against America'.

Mentor of Alice Bailey was a 'Georgian' but, not a great-grandmother and she was not from Georgia in America.

GOD confirmed I needed to rest in Him.

Then, when rested, seek more truth together.

Wow!

God revealed the status within moments after He arranged a special time of rest. More repentance since I spent so much time and effort being sure I had the right information from trusted sources!

Yikes! Our Father was clear: I trusted long term sources were automatically legitimate news sources. Due diligence in what appeared to be the right sources is what took me down rabbit trails – KKK – Iowa connections – David Duke – all bunny trails which wasted time within 'news sources which were supposed to be reliable'. Our LORD then revealed that I ignored a source which seemed questionable while I forgot many news sources are actually 'fake news'. Wow! I had to shift gears to realign with our Father!

GOD re-directed my attention to specific personal letters given to a blog and a web site. The people in charge of the news sites received the truth from a man directly involved within the Elberton Philomathea # 25 Masonic Lodge during the time frame of the deal being arranged for the Georgia Guidestones. The man provided letters with the facts clearly outlined shortly before he died.

The man confirmed exactly what took place with the members of Philomathea # 25 Masonic Lodge who were directly involved in the deal. He also named two men in the Lodge who were not in agreement with the Guidestones. The two men were removed from the Masonic Lodge. The series of letters were presented to the man or group of men involved in the blog and web site headquartered in north west Georgia, a significant distance from Elberton.

GOD confirmed the names and details regarding the local people who were directly involved in the deal and that they were aware of the truth which is stated in the letters. The source for the letters actually passed away shortly after he shared the specifics. Grateful the letters confirm the same facts shared within the blog and 'in letter form' on the web site:

An elegant, silver haired man made the deal.

The man stated up front he was using a pseudonym.

Bank still processed 'a check' from the anonymous source.

TRUTH: The man declared he was and the letters confirm the man is still famous. The man is a well known business man in America and he owns significant businesses headquartered in Atlanta, Georgia. Immediately, I researched his background. When he was young, his family moved to Savannah, Georgia and he has remained in Georgia.

Because he is the one still living, I'm not inserting his name but, he is recognized for founding multiple news networks, both radio and TV. He is especially well known for a world famous TV cable news network within his well known broadcasting system which is more famous now due to becoming known as the news networks which President Trump refers to as 'fake news'.

Very important to note that this man owns multiple news networks within his personal structure under his personal broadcasting system title.

When was the global news network launched? June 1, 1980, a coincidence it was the date when Alice Bailey would have been 100 years old (June 1880-1980).

He is also identified as a 33rd degree Mason in the Order of Malta. **What is the Order of Malta?** Sovereign Military Society, a subject of International Law.

In addition, this man is also well known for donating one billion dollars to the United Nations to establish the United Nations Foundation.

What is the United Nations Foundation?

It is a public charity which was founded <u>for the specific purpose of broadening domestic support of the United Nations</u>.

He became the Chairman the day it was founded and he remains as the Chairman of the foundation to this day.

How is this man connected with R C Christian?

There are ties between this man and a close colleague who is the man specifically identified in the letters of the pseudonym R C Christian, a man listed as a co-worker on the Guidestones deal within the exact same letters letters used: R C C.

The second man is Robert Clark Cook (R C C).

Both of the men are involved in the Eugenics Society which was founded by Robert Cook, a geneticist. Cook knew Josef Mengele personally. Cook's work was reported as being used for the selection of who lived and who died in the German Holocaust during World War II.

Georgia Guidestones plan is exactly the same.

Cook was involved but, at 80 years old, he was not the man who arranged the deal with the granite company owner, the bank president or the land owner.

According to the man providing a letter about the 'deal' for the Guidestones, the man arranging the deal said his partner (R C Cook) actually lived in the Elberton area and he would be the one checking on the progress. However, according to Cook's obituary, Cook lived in a senior community in North Carolina. No mention of a connection to Elberton, Georgia or Georgia in his obituary.

The Elbert County Board of Commissioners became responsible for checking on the progress and maintaining the stones and the land.

Interesting fact: Cook is represented within the use of his exact same initials as R C Christian, the name allowed as a pseudonym since it was supposedly required as an anonymous name to protect the true identity of the man who entered the bank to arrange the deal with Wyatt Martin, President of the bank.

Why? The man stated he was well known but, he must remain anonymous.

Background of R C Cook:

Cook was a geneticist.

He was the founder and leader of the American Eugenics Society, directly involved with Planned Parenthood and the Association for Research in Human Heredity.

Cook authored: *"Human Fertility: The Modern Dilemma."*

In 1955 he was a co-recipient of the Albert and Mary Lasker Foundation's **planned parenthood award** for his *"outstanding contribution to wider understanding of the world population problem."* Facts can be obtained direct from his obituary.

Interesting to note that Margaret Sanger (1879-1966), founder of Planned Parenthood, devoted her life to legalizing birth control. She founded the American Birth Control League 100 years ago, an entity which evolved into Planned Parenthood. Her work spread across the nation and it went global before her death in 1966. Birth control pills were already issued and *Zero Population Growth* was a program shared on college campuses across the nation.

Sanger was also involved in the Eugenics Society and a close colleague of Robert Clark Cook.

The Theosophical Society and the Eugenics Society follow the reasoning of Thomas Paine who wrote *The Age Of Reason.*

Remember the Guidestones message which is carved into the four sides of the capstone, in the four ancient languages?

Let these be Guidestones to an Age of Reason.

Who translated the languages on the Guidestones?

Staff within the United Nations.

1. Maintain humanity under 500,000,000 in perpetual balance with nature.

2. Guide reproduction wisely – improving fitness and diversity.

3. Unite humanity with a living new language.

4. Rule passion – faith – tradition – and all things with tempered reason.

5. Protect people and nations with fair laws and just courts.

6. Let all nations rule internally resolving external disputes in a world court.

7. Avoid petty laws and useless officials.

8. Balance personal rights with social duties.

9. Prize truth – beauty – love – seeking harmony with the infinite.

10. Be not a cancer on the earth – Leave room for nature – Leave room for nature.

Truth:

The stones are positioned exactly according to Baal worship, sun worship. The details can easily be researched.

The diagram of the exact positioning of the stones is provided for your information, only, because it is also available within the exact same format on a few web sites, i.e., beyond concept, vigilant citizen, etc.

Georgia Guidestones

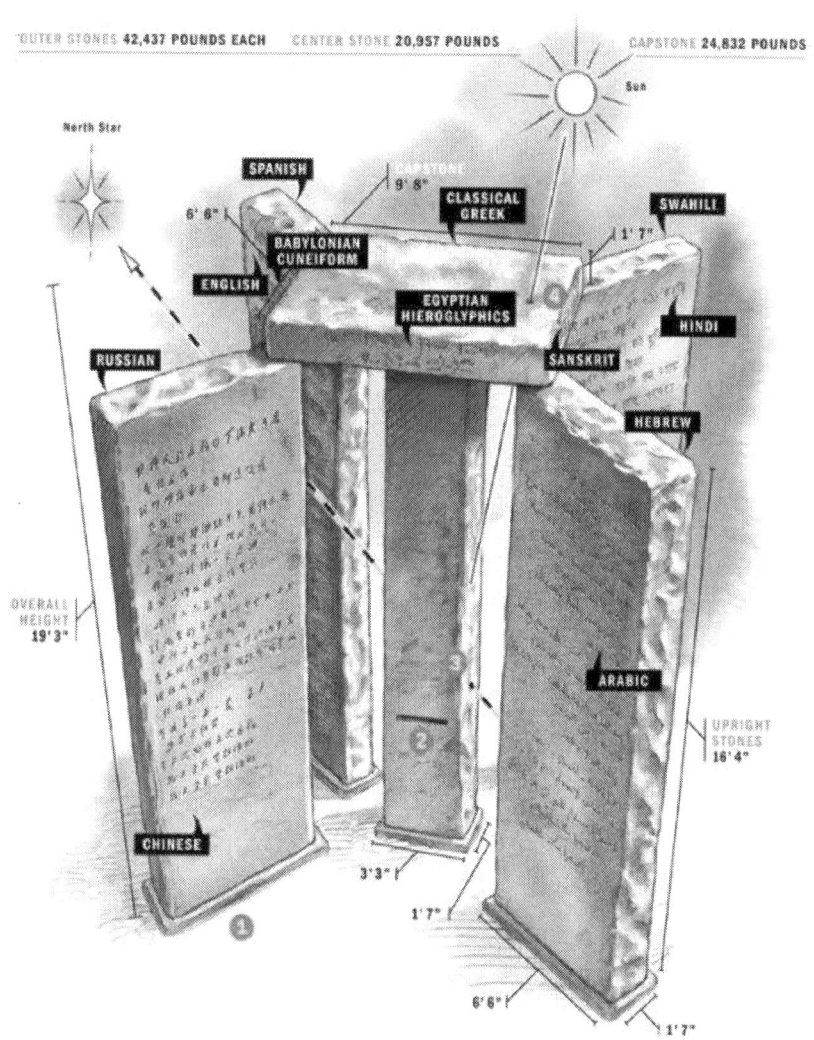

The reason for each hole drilled and each stone placement is specific to movements of the sun, Baal, sun worship.

Directing you to the web sites since I am not interested in discussing or focusing time and energy upon revealing any sun worship details.

If you have an opportunity to visit the Guidestones I trust the LORD will prompt you to observe but, **do not touch**.

Why? Curses are real.

Important to use discernment. Thank our Father for granting you discernment! **Warning to disciples: Prosecutions Are Coming. Matthew 10:16.** *"Behold, I send you out as sheep in the midst of wolves. Therefore be wise as serpents and harmless as doves.* (Continues as a powerful message until verse 20). We have learned how to be 'harmless as doves' at all times and love all so 'those sent on assignment' know they can proceed. Thank you LORD for doing whatever it takes to help each one in the body of believers to gain discernment, know what we are dealing with and do whatever it requires to remain aligned with You at all times.

Evil exists and it is 'at work' in the world.

In all things, seek God's guidance.

He will confirm if it is for us to deal with or not because taking on evil requires full submission to our Father, to operate in His strength when we are faced with evil.

If we enter into battle and we are not ready, the enemy already knows! Do not attempt to operate in your own power. This is not a reflection of any one of us for we each need to pray and prepare by seeking God's truth before we proceed. Even top leaders in the body of Christ operate within their own power at times. You can tell the difference, when they return from a trip and have to be met at the plane with a wheelchair and left alone for days after their trip to rest from their 'travel for God'. Truth is GOD energizes, handles the matter and restores us after each encounter and we return to share the testimonies far & wide.

The world-based plan is not filled with blessings for GOD's people. It is clear to ALL who have ears to hear us for we are either cursing or blessing and we are either receiving curses or blessings.

Georgia Guidestones were established in 1980, nearly 100 years after the Faith Monument was dedicated in 1889. Residents across America do not know the Faith Monument exists and most of the residents even in Elberton, Georgia and many in Georgia do not know the Guidestones exist.

Remember the changes in 100 years shared in *For The Sake Of America II?*

Jonah went to Nineveh, described in Jonah 4.

Nineveh was given the privilege of knowing the one true GOD. Under Jonah's preaching this great Gentile city had repented, and GOD had graciously stayed His judgment.

Nahum was prompted by God to go to Nineveh 100 years later.

Nahum proclaims the downfall of this city: "The Assyrians have forgotten their revival and have returned to their habits of violence, idolatry, and arrogance. As a result, Babylon will so destroy the city that no trace of it will remain" – a prophecy fulfilled in painful detail.

LORD we repent! Thank You for keeping Your hand upon us for we have become a nation which reflects the enemy: living in fear, doubt and unbelief with many stealing, killing and destroying. We have taken over the land and made it ours while it is YOUR land, Father, and we are only here temporary to share the abundance You provide. Forgive us! We have not aligned together as believers, aligned 100% with Your will, while standing firm in faith and proclaiming Your word and Your truth. We have compromised with the world plan over time and therefore, we have forgotten our First Love, our Redeemer, our Savior, our Christ, our Yeshua Hamashiach!

Forgive us LORD for ALL that has been done against Your purpose and plan for our lives in these days. We repent and ask the Holy Spirit to fill every hole, heal every wound and speak Your words of truth to us NOW!

Chapter 4   Native Indian History, Significance to America

Research says: Lies have been repeated for more than 200 years as truth. Will we repent for the lies? Will we seek the truth?

Native Indians were protected with proclamations and treaties. The treaties were to assure the Indians that they were not going to be removed from their land! That was not the truth in many areas. Fraudulent treaties were tried in court. Indians won the cases but, their homes and land were already sold to plantation owners.

'Indian Wars' are still being stated as wars 'to this day' due to the fact they had to fight for their land every time settlers arrived and staked their claim on land which was 'set aside' for Indians.

These wars continued for more than 100 years after the forced removal from their homes and land, 1804 - late 1820's, until 1920!

Wiseman Memorial

God prompted me to remember what I was told as a child about the Wiseman Memorial near the Missouri River. The father was serving in the Cavalry. The mother left the children to travel two days each way to obtain supplies from stores in Yankton, South Dakota. In part, the long journey was due to having to cross the Missouri River. While the mother was gone, the story told to everyone at the time, and in a book prepared by the family, is that Native Indians entered and killed the children in the home.

The anger toward the Native Indians was not understood then, or since. The anger was displayed as though the anger Indians expressed as portrayed in movies and TV programs was real. What was the premise of every story? Indians were repeatedly killing settlers. Why was it confusing? Indian land became the land offered to new pioneers, settlers upon the land, by the government.

Not once did anyone question why the Indians did not show up at any other home in the entire region along the Missouri River even though families lived in each section of land in the region!

Nobody shared the truth about the Wiseman family.

What was the truth?

The father, Henson Wiseman, was actively involved in taking away land from the Native Indians. In the process, Native Indian women and children were killed while the men of the tribe(s) were hunting to provide for their families while protecting their territory.

The four Native Indians which sought out the home of Wiseman were very aware it was the exact home of the same man responsible for killing entire families of their tribe(s).

No other families were attacked. None of this information appears within the books sold regarding the Wiseman Memorial.

The 'massacre' happened 150 years before God sent me to Georgia in 2013, July 24, 1863. When I visited the site & local museum in 2015, the woman behind the counter in the gift shop wanted me to know how terrible it was to think about the horrific things the Native Indians did to the children of the Wiseman family. I asked her if she knew the truth about the position the father of the children held in the Cavalry. She was not aware.

Native Indians were granted territories for their tribes / tribal nations. Then, land was granted to settlers in a 'land rush' process coordinated through the government. Settlers were able to stake their claim on land granted to the Indians. All of this was taking place without consistent communication available. The Native Indians were being placed on smaller and smaller parcels of land identified within specific reservations which were promised to be protected by the Federal Government.

The journey has not been smooth for me while releasing the truth because we have been encased in lies for so many generations. Without realizing it, people have attacked me about the truth by merely repeating the lies, facts which they cannot prove but they accept as truth. Even though I provide the truth and the facts, it is sad to report to you that they typically refuse to stop repeating the lies! *LORD forgive us!*

Research has been extensive! Why is it so tough to get to the truth? A lot of effort was put into making the lies sound good, to keep the lies sounding right, as though they were the truth.

GOD had to reveal the truth to me during each phase of the journey in Georgia because I did not know the lies were lies, either.

After *For The Sake Of America II* was released, GOD reminded me that I did not research the Hebrew meaning of the word Indian before the book was released.

GOD wanted me to refer more to 'Hebrew meanings' which is why GOD arranged for Bill and Gwen Morford to gift me with the book: *Fulfillment of Prophecy* by Eliezer Ben-Yehuda. When Eliezer was told by well meaning doctors that his life would end soon, GOD prompted him to study and provide Hebrew for people to know the truth about the language. The famous quote by Eliezer confirms the truth GOD prompted him to reveal to us: *The two things without which the Jews will not be a nation: The Land and the Language.*

NOTE: We have not protected our language.

Example: Los Angeles already prints documents in **Chinese, Cambodian/Khmer, Farsi, Korean, Spanish, Tagalog/Filipino, Vietnamese, Hindi, Japanese, Thai and Russian.** California election documents are 'required by law, Section 14201' to be provided in multiple languages, county by county. In fact, six new languages are being added 'per law' to the 2018 election documents: **Panjabi (Punjabi), Hmong, Syriac, Armenian, Persian and Arabic.**

Clearly, I did not realize the depth of the meaning of the words in Hebrew and perhaps this request by GOD continued since the readers of *For The Sake Of America II* knew there was more to the story. They knew the second book led them to a third book. This was very odd to me, since I wrote the second book with our LORD and there was not a plan to proceed with a third book!

Now, I am repenting for what I did regarding our Father's request to research the word Indian in Hebrew since I realize now that before shifting my mind into gear, I quickly responded my reluctance to proceed upon the request due to the fact it appeared to me that the word Indian was English and it was merely a name added by the new people who came to the land in the 1800's.

Declaration before God and all others:

> *I was wrong!*

> *Now, I repented!*

In **Hebrew,** the word for **Indian** is **Amit (Hebrew: עמית)** and it means **a friend,** a **person of Israel origin.**

The Native Indians were friends to all who came. They shared the land and all products from their labor. Plus, they shared all tools and resources. They knew the truth as stated in **Psalms 24** and **I Corinthians 10:26.** *The earth* (land) *is the LORD's and the fullness thereof.*

The truth was passed on generation to generation for nearly 2300 years by the tribes of Israel from about 500 BC until the early

1800's AD in America, until the Native Indians were forced out of their homes and off their land, actions which continued until the Native Indian Removal Act was passed. The Native Indians proceed to the Supreme Court with a Georgia case and won but, they were not able to enforce the truth. They were forced to leave with the full knowledge of the truth, the tears they shed were due to realizing the depth of the enmity being created between the 'new settlers, plantation owners and the only Creator'.

They knew what they were doing when they piled stones along the Nation line between the Cherokee and Creek Nations.

They knew the significance of the **Stones of Remembrance** confirming the truth *'we shall always remember what happened here and what our GOD did to provide all of this for us'*.

We have a lot to learn and therefore, a lot to repent for as people who claim to be 'joint heirs' with Christ and the land!

Remember what the Native Americans and Pilgrims gave us?

1 Faith Monument, the structure which is required for us to follow so we would be able to remain in liberty and freedom.

2 Structure of our founding documents for the initial colonies and then the states, with Congress paying for all of the costs to print and disburse the first bibles to every church, school and home.

The plan was simple.

The purpose was clear.

What did they give us?

✓ The Faith Monument

The Faith Monument is a granite monument dedicated in 1889, located within a residential community above Plymouth Rock. Faith Monument stands 81 feet tall and weighs several ton.

Our Congress paid for the Faith Monument.

The monument includes the structure we are to follow to retain Freedom and Liberty.

LIE: Georgia Guidestones monument is claimed to be the tallest, biggest granite monument with slabs 19 feet, 3 inches tall. They are not quite one-fourth the height of the Faith Monument. Georgia Guidestones also claim to use the most granite at under 300,000 pounds.

Truth: The Faith Monument took 70 years to complete and the weight is several ton. The truth was known about the Faith Monument for an entire century before the Guidestones were unveiled in 1980, more than 90 years after the Faith Monument was dedicated, 100 years after it was established.

Faith Monument

Faith monument includes four separate sections which display images confirming exactly how we can proceed to retain our liberty and freedom:

At the top: **Faith**. She points to Heaven, to our Creator. She is holding an open bible, the basis of our faith.

The four pillars at the foundation of the **Faith Monument:**

1. Morality is holding the Ten Commandments in her left hand and the scroll of revelation in her right hand. At the base of the throne are the engravings: **Evangelist** and **Prophecy.** She has no eyes. She looks inward because liberty must be in us before it will show up within the nation.

2. Law founded upon the bible, the source of truth as the Pilgrims **General Laws** confirm: *...by how much they (the laws) are derived from, and agreeable to the ancient Platform of God's Law."* The two carved items under the throne where **Law** is seated represent **Justice** and **Mercy.**

3. Education is holding an open book of knowledge, the Bible. Her throne has two carvings: **Youth** receiving instruction and

Wisdom represented by a grandfather who points to the bible while standing a globe, confirming both parents and grandparents are to teach the youth from a Biblical perspective. She is wearing a **Victory** wreath for focusing the youth upon the truth and the way to proceed in their life, resulting in the *training up a child in the way he shall go so when he is old he will not depart from it* as confirmed within **Proverbs 22:6.**

4. Liberty is seated with a sword in his hand. He is prepared to protect the family and liberty. Two carvings: **Tyranny** and **Peace.** The images clearly confirm why the Pilgrims / Puritans were known as the *Parents of America, the Republic* confirmed by the the Founding Fathers.

Constitutional Convention

As the Founding Fathers were leaving the Constitutional Convention in Philadelphia, Mrs. Powell asked a simple question: *What have you given us Dr Franklin?* She received a simple response from Benjamin Franklin: *A Republic, if you can keep it.*

The plan to retain America as a Republic is confirmed in our founding documents and the Pledge of Allegiance: *... and to the Republic for which it* (the flag) *stands.* A Republic government is of, by and for the people. Each citizen has rights as a sovereign. In a Democracy, rights are granted to and secured by majority rule which often becomes mob rule.

When the people fear the government there is tyranny,

when the government fears the people there is liberty.

Quote by Thomas Jefferson

The constitutional convention is important to Georgia with a key person participating who would make a huge difference within the future plans from Macon, Georgia to Moravian Falls, North Carolina. The exact location God identified *For The Sake Of America* when GOD released the word to the prophets.

Important to realize the connection between these details of pushing the Indians south of the Ohio River and then, deciding to sell the reduced acreage of land belonging to the Native Indians to the cotton plantations coming south from North and South Carolina into Georgia. This is the exact location of what GOD confirmed to the three prophets in the vision which made the location so critical to America. They were crying out for America when our Father confirmed that He has positioned angelic vortexes over Macon, Georgia and Moravian Falls, North Carolina *For The Sake Of America.*

There is a strong push across America now by groups who are united in their belief that another Constitutional Convention needs to be held as the Constitution has to be changed.

We need to remain in prayer with our Father in these days!

The man attending the Constitutional Convention from Georgia was **Benjamin Hawkins. Hawkins** served as the US Agent to the Native Indians, reporting directly to President George Washington.

He was able to keep the peace with all of the Native Indians from the beginning of our nation and for more than two decades. He was the US Agent who negotiated treaties with the Native Indians for forts and land acquisition to secure the nation through battles after we gained our independence as a nation.

Generally recognized as an Indian 'agent', Benjamin Hawkins held the title of General Superintendent of all tribes south of the Ohio River for more than two decades. Fort Hawkins on a high ridge in Macon, Georgia is located within the original town of Hawkinsville which is part of Macon, Georgia to this day.

Hawkins was well respected as the overseer of the longest period of peace with the Creek Nation, only to watch his lifetime of work destroyed by a small faction of this Indian Nation known as the 'Red Sticks' during the War of 1812 which was being fought against the British.

The 1812 war with the British started and ended in 1812 and that is all we heard about the War of 1812.

However, the 'Red Sticks' war extended through 1813 and 1814, a fact we do not hear about within our national history. This war was conducted with the Native Indians using red colored clubs and this is how the Native Indians were later referred to as redskins. Their skin was not red in color. Their use of war paint and the clubs during the war were red in color.

Baldwin (aka Stonepile), Georgia

Where were the stones piled in Baldwin, Georgia? In the center of town, specifically at the line between the Creek and Cherokee nations. This location is also known as the Continental Divide. Plus, the location is also known as the **"Hawkins Line"** due to the location representing the place where a treaty with the Cherokee nation was signed by the government, an agreement for peace which was arranged by Hawkins in 1804.

Structure of America

The truth is: Pilgrims and the Jews from Spain were already united with the Hebrews, the Native Americans.

They knew how to live in peace on the land for 200 and 300+ years already.

They are credited with the wording of the documents for establishing the initial structure for the states and ... *they colonized many of the states.*

Laws were established from the Ten Commandments.

More than half of the Founding Fathers and the signers of the Declaration of Independence were seminary graduates!

Signers of the Declaration were also representing the Colonies and then States in Congress and personally funded the printing of the first bibles. These facts are within research done by David Barton.

Bradford Quote. On the Faith Monument, a special quote from William Bradford speaks to the depth of faith, knowledge, and wisdom in the people we refer to as Pilgrims or Puritans:

Thus out of small beginnings greater things have been produced by His hand that made all things of nothing and gives being to all things that are, and as one small candle may light a thousand, so the light here kindled hath shone unto many, yea in some sort to our whole nation, let the glorious name of Jehovah have all praise.

Bradford focused all praise on the Hebrew name of our LORD, the Father, Jehovah our Yahweh, Yah or Y-h (vowels not used), the praises to the one true and only living GOD (G-D). Hallelujah means 'praise be to Yah', God be praised, the worship of Jehovah / Yahweh, Yah.

With everything based upon the Word, the Bible, and the exact details being provided to keep a nation free and a people living in liberty, how could a blessed nation return to the traditions of pagan worship and the pagan rituals of Christmas and Easter?

Instead of following our Hebrew calendar which includes the structure the LORD put in place, we denied the truth after receiving so many benefits from the Christian standard set in America by the Pilgrims / Puritans.

Over time, what did we do?

We aligned with stories we heard without researching the facts because the depth of the stories are a shock! Facts shared were not based upon truth. We merely repeated the stories again and again, generation to generation. Then, we wanted generations to 'do better in the world than prior generations'. Now, we wonder how the current generation appears to be 'so far off the mark'. We did this!

It's a sad status for us today, especially since the Hebrews were granted the land and lived free on the land under Divine Law for more than 2300 years. Pilgrims knew the truth and sacrificed everything to come to this land of America with a 500 year plan, a plan for our success as a people until at least 2020. It was a plan which worked beautifully for about 200 to 250 years. Then, 'new people' changed everything with the Native Indian Removal Act after they already took over the homes and land and placed land into personal deeds 'for a fee paid to the new government'.

LORD forgive us!

Would be nice to know what it would be like if we would have continued upon the 500 year plan! We would have bypassed the debacles created by removing the Native people from their homes and land and we would still be proceeding upon the plan for another 100 years!

There is a strong push for a new, Continental Congress to establish a new Constitution.

More repentance and prayer required!

Cherokee Nation, Significance to America

Cherokee are often identified as the **Issachar Tribe.**

This tribe is one of the lost tribes of Israel, sons of Jacob/Israel.

The first time I heard the initial details about the Cherokee people and how much we owe them since they actually preserved the Hebrew language, and if they had not then the true name of our heavenly Father would be lost, I admit I was skeptical. In fact, I was absolutely stunned. Everything I heard was 'all new' to me!

The journey our Yahweh, Hebrew name preserved by Cherokee (originally identified as Ya-hu-wah), arranged for me throughout Georgia has helped me clearly understand the 'depth of disbelief' people have expressed, especially due to how the 'lies shared generation to generation were accepted as 100% truth over time'.

To begin, we have to use 20/20 hindsight:

This 'encased in a web of deceit' status inspires me to listen so closely to our Father that I can hear his heartbeat, to continue to go where God needs me to go, to do what He needs me to do to be 'in position, aligned with His will' to seek out and share HIS truth.

Hopefully, the truth will help us begin to understand how this blessed nation of Yahweh was given to the 'original people', a nation which existed in peace for more than 2000 years before 1492 when Cristobal Colon, from a Jewish family with roots back to his Jewish lineage in Italy (changed his name to Christopher Columbus while living in Spain), arrived and named this land America 'for Spain' with money stolen from Jewish families.

The original people (lost tribes of Israel) knew the truth about this land when they observed our Father taking up all of the water so they were able to travel by foot for a year and a half to the new, uninhabited land. This fact is specifically described within the Apocrypha.

The people were specifically given 'an uninhabited land' within about 200 years of their capture and removal from Israel by the King of Assyria in 721 BC. The closest placement we can provide for their arrival is about 500 BC, since the etching of the Ten Commandments by the Cherokee, found in New Mexico, is described as being etched on stone in Paleo Hebrew of 500 BC.

After *For The Sake Of America II* was released, the questions about the Cherokee nation were significant.

Some people absolutely denied the Cherokee nation had a connection with God. They were wrong!

In the midst of the debate, Heather Rock offered more proof:

Cherokee Artifact, not identified
Cherokee Museum in Cherokee, North Carolina

Enlargement of Stone Artifact

<u>Stone</u>: Praise be to Yah, Hallelujah, 10th Century BC Paleo Hebrew

Heather Rock journeyed to Cherokee, North Carolina to the Cherokee Museum. Staff had no idea what the artifact meant and therefore, there is no description provided within the shadow box on display.

When Heather mentioned books which confirm the first slaves in America were the black Native American Indians, people who were considered as the original black people, the first black slaves, it was absolutely a complete surprise.

Were the black slaves only Cherokee? **NO!**

During my time in Georgia, I have met many people of Cherokee, Blackfoot and Creek descent.

They know their ancestors were enslaved.

Female, Cherokee Chief

They know their families were 'ripped apart'.

They know the parents, especially the fathers, were removed from the families and their children were placed in foster care to be adopted by new settlers. Many of the children were also enslaved, and they were placed in government or public schools for their English education.

The people I have met have various skin colors from light to dark, even though they are unaware of their heritage due to the stories being passed, they have heard the truth passed on 'by the elders' from generation to generation. However, many ancestors were killed for sharing the truth so they chose to merely hold on to the truth and pass it on to the current and future generations.

People considered to be black in color made up the majority of the slave trade while not all slaves were black. It is true that a few were brought from Africa while many if not all of the slaves from Africa were also Hebrew and knew the same 'stories' shared by the Native Indians in America. *LORD forgive us!*

It is heartbreaking to hear the stories from people who have become close friends when they describe their lineage with a foster grandfather, a foster great-grandfather, a foster great-great-grandfather on both sides of their family! Plus, no records to refer to because the court houses were burned during the Civil War.

The tribe known as Cherokee has submitted to DNA testing and the tests have confirmed the tribe is from the tribe of Issachar, one of the lost tribes of North Israel.

This time, I followed every prompting of our Father to research everything 'for the meaning in the Hebrew'.

What a difference!

So, who was Issachar as the son of Jacob?

> *Number 9 son.*

What does the number nine mean in Hebrew?

> *Two sides, good and evil:*
>> *Pain in childbirth but, leads to a new life.*
> *Those who accomplish the divine will.*
> *Expanded patience; perfect movement of God.*

What does the name Issachar mean?

> *'Man of hire'.*

Why was he given this name?

> *'Leah hired Jacob for the night; Leah arranged with Rachel to be with Jacob for the night'.*

91

How was he addressed within the family?

A donkey.

Why did Issachar receive this casual nickname?

Again, 'man of labor' … 'man of hire' …

'a carrier of burdens'.

Did Jacob speak a blessing over Issachar?

Yes.

In Hebrew for Christians, Jacob's blessing is stated to be something like this:

Issachar is a strong donkey,

Lying down between two burdens;

He saw that the rest was good,

And that the land was pleasant;

He bowed his shoulder to bear a burden,

And became a band of slaves.

The wisdom of the Cherokee warrior was evident to the government in America.

In fact, in 2007 God arranged a meeting 'just for me' to attend a one-on-one with a Cherokee tribal leader a few days before God sent me to Kuala Lumpur, Malaysia. In shock when I heard the testimonies from travel the Cherokee leader was required to do 'as a ghost' for the government.

Personally, I had no idea what he meant when he said he traveled as 'a ghost' for the government but, within moments his testimonies made the status he was describing very clear.

This meeting took place more than ten years ago and I did not realize the significance at the time God arranged my personal connection with this amazing tribal Chief and man of God until now. God's divine orchestration is beyond comprehension.

What is a ghost?

The Cherokee leader was born and raised 'in seclusion' on a military base exactly as his immediate family (father) and ancestors (grandfathers) were held for many generations.

When the government needed him to identify and remove a 'target' on behalf of the government, he was sent on the mission. If he was killed and did not return, another Cherokee warrior would be sent as a 'ghost'. If he returned, he would merely be given another assignment. Government did not appear to realize 'divine protection' as the reason why the 'ghost' was able to return, again and again and again until he was of an age to retire; age made it difficult to continue.

All I knew at the time of our conversation was that I was being highly blessed! His prayers for my divine protection in Malaysia helped me tremendously. God knew what I did not know. I was only a few days away from entering the fully Muslim nation of Malaysia. Plus, the day of my arrival was the exact day of the beginning of their Muslim high holy days of Ramadan!

GOD has a tremendous sense of humor!

Issachar tribe became the tribe filled with leaders, they became very successful on the land, and so prosperous as a tribal nation. In fact, they rose to third tribe of the twelve tribes in Israel.

Enslavement. Only the Cherokee? **No.**

The Native Indians were enslaved long before some people from Africa were brought to America and included within the slave trade. The original tribes of Israel, the Native Indians, were on the land for centuries before it was called America. They were dark in color, not red. There are several books about their lives, book which confirm the Native tribes were the first black slaves.

Redskins. How did American Indians gain the title?

When the War of 1812 was extended due to the upset of a few of the **Creek** Indians (recognized as the Israel tribe of **Manasseh**), men who were fighting with red colored sticks. The Red Sticks became famous in news articles. The few were fighting due to the fact they were being removed from their homes and their land. The majority did not fight. Sad status for those who followed the new legal process established by the new settlers on the land because they were not successful. The plans to remove the Native Indians were already in process. Plans gained momentum due to the option to sell the land to new settlers by re-locating cotton plantations from North and South Carolina.

People who were identified as Native Indians were called Redskins after the war. The fight with red sticks by some of the Creek Nation became the root of the phrase repeated to this day: *God willing and the Creek don't rise!*

They were people who followed God's will. The uprising was created by a few who refused to accept that their homes and lands could be stolen by the new people arriving on the land.

Truth not understood, again!

The majority did not fight or want their people to fight since it would create enmity between them and the LORD, the Great Spirit, Creator of all. They lived according to Divine Law and they helped structure the laws on the land. This was and is the truth.

Within twelve years, however, the new people on the land pursued the removal of the Native Indians.

The Cherokee pursued a case to present the truth to the courts. They pursued their case all the way to the Supreme Court. The Cherokee won but, President Andrew Jackson knew the Supreme Court Justice could not enforce it. Therefore, the Native Indians were forced to leave Georgia and proceed on the Trail of Tears to Oklahoma. Tears they shed due to what was being done 'against the Creator', as they knew Jehovah, Yahweh would take care of them.

Pride and greed took over!

Land could be sold to cotton plantations for great sums of cash and the work could be done by the original people 'who lived free on the land and allowed all who came to enjoy the abundance of crops and resources provided by the Creator and to enjoy the same rights and freedom'!

However, the new people felt 'entitled', pride and greed took over!

Discovering gold in Georgia played a big part in the Native Indian Removal Act being passed so quickly.

It was the Cherokee who fought the Native Indian Removal Act.

They took the case through the court in Georgia and continued all the way to the United States Supreme Court.

They won!

Their victory was not honored.

The plan to remove them was already in place and the momentum was increasing by the day.

The Native Indians actually took their people to the new courts when they were involved in actions against the new settlers and their new laws. The Native Indians agreed with the decisions of the courts when their people were prosecuted, served terms or were put to death based upon the outcome of the legal decisions.

Peace continued.

The Native Indians knew they lived under Divine Law.

They knew they did not want to allow anything which would case enmity between them and the LORD.

Gold had been discovered in Georgia in 1828, resulting in a Democrat-controlled Congress rushing through the Indian Removal Act, which passed by a single vote in 1830. It was signed by Democrat President Andrew Jackson and carried out by Democrat President Martin Van Buren.

Important to note: It was not a 'native people' act, it was specifically an Indian (people of Israel origin) Removal Act. Cherokee submitted a case against Georgia proceeding immediately with their removal from their homes and land due to the Indian Removal Act. The case was taken all the way to the Supreme Court.

Chief Justice John Marshall ruled in favor of the Cherokee in Worcester v. Georgia (1832), writing that *the Cherokee Nation was a "distinct community" with self-government "in which the laws of Georgia can have no force."*

He (also) said, *"Thanks be to GOD, the Court can wash their hands clean of the iniquity of oppressing the Indians and disregarding their rights."*

This was a case which the Cherokee clearly won and yet, President Andrew Jackson would not enforce the ruling and no enforcement resulted in no option for the Indians and this played a big part.

What happened to the people who heard the truth from the Indians and knew they were the lost tribes of Israel?
Ministers and missionaries who fought for the truth to be revealed were actually imprisoned and forced into labor camps.

The Native Indians were living in complete peace for more than 2300 years. Then, everything changed due to allowing hundreds of thousands of

other people to enter the nation and change everything about their life.

Everything changed quickly after the original people lived in complete harmony with the people who came. First arrivals knew who the original people were and they lived in peace 'on the land' for more than two hundred and three hundred years!

The Pilgrims came with the specific 500 year plan.

The Pilgrims and the Native Indians, including the people who arrived in 1492, helped structure the State documents from their participation during the development of the Colonies, through the Revolutionary War, the development of the Constitution and Declaration of Independence. They knew the structure our LORD desired due to operating under Divine Law prior to the 1700's.

Staggering thought.

Time to reflect and see where we are now, compared to where the tribes of Israel were for about 2300 years before the forced removal from their homes and land in the early 1800's!

HISTORY:

The people already 'on the land' allowed the new people to come, share in the resources and crops while they taught the new people how to live off the land for there was an abundance for all to enjoy.

After more than 2300 years of peace, within about 50 years, the new people arrived and took over the land, removed the native residents from their homes and land, removed the native children from their parents, enslaved them, killed them and removed the original people from the only region of the country they knew.

CURRENT DAY:

The potential of the current status of America experiencing a repeat of history is high due to millions of people entering the nation, immediately declaring / demanding rights of legal citizens, demanding their culture and laws are to be honored, demands which are changing laws to laws which are not aligned with the laws of the land.

They are arriving without documentation, without medical records, bringing medical issues back to the land which were already eradicated. Now, lawsuits are being pursued because the children crossing the border are being given shots and medicine. Americans are imprisoned for arriving without proper shots and medicine (malaria, etc.). We are already seeing the impact upon the people currently owning homes and residing upon the land?

Blending of Israelites and Jews
2000 years after Arrival of the Lost Tribes of Israel

Jewish people who were forced to leave Spain embarked upon their journey the exact same day as Columbus because they knew the truth about the day to travel and about the land in 1492 AD.

Blending of Israelites, Jews & Pilgrims
2100 years after Arrival of the Lost Tribes of Israel

The Pilgrims sacrificed everything based upon knowing the truth, as provided within the 1611 King James bible, before they chose to depart and continue their efforts during extreme, dire circumstances to get to this land in 1620.

The peace was maintained while the Pilgrims settled into life about 2100 years after the native people established life on the uninhabited land.

Blending of Israelites, Jews, Pilgrims & Patriots
2200 years after Arrival of the Lost Tribes of Israel

All of the 'new people' coming to the land named America about 2200 years after the original people arrived, operated in peace. In less than 100 years, everything changed! When the first Europeans arrived and fought for this land to be an independent land, the native people, Jews and Pilgrims aligned with them without knowing the plans would quickly change.

It causes 'pause' to realize the harmony established over the centuries, the peace held by all of the people, resulted in an abrupt halt within less than 60 years as a new nation of America structured into States, gaining new land or territory.

How did it go so wrong, so fast?
Pride and greed have many layers!
Greed and pride played a big part!
Money for land belonging to God played a big part!

Oglethorpe bringing the debtor's prison inmates to the 'new land' to become 'the settlers of the land' and then after interviewing the 'inmates' Oglethorpe changed his plan and brought land owners to Georgia who became land barons and that played a big part!

Title deeds to land, land which the Native Indians knew belonged only to the LORD, the Creator, caused division because the Native Indians lived under Divine Law for more than 2200 years until new cultures and plans were developed and this change played a big part!

A photo was shared by an anonymous source as humor. However, will it become true about the land in America as it did with the land in Israel?

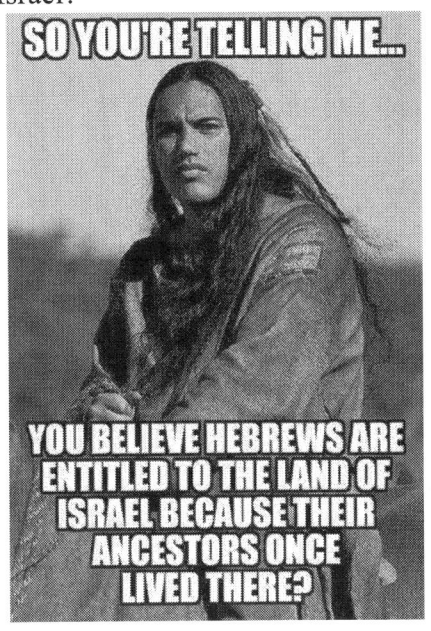

The pride and greed 'went global'.

Nations were taken over by worldly empires, i.e., France, Spain, British Empire, proceeded to establish colonies globally by following the same pattern established on a land recognized as a blessed land, a land titled as America.

Gold mines, diamond mines, resources belonging to Yahweh, preserved by the Native People were taken over by 'conquerors'.

LORD help us repent for all, known and unknown in this hour so the captives can be set free!

Help us to seek and know your truth!

Help us to know who we are as a family member You have grafted in to the eternal family!

Help us to love all You love!

Help us to forgive as deeply as you forgive!

Help us to know who we are as the truth, the word carriers, true representatives, Ambassadors for Christ, so we can represent you in truth and reach all who have not heard the truth.

Chapter 5   Savannah, Georgia Significance to America

Met an amazing man of God during a rushed trip to Wisconsin in December 2012. Yes. Wisconsin in December. Yes. I agree. I had the exact same thought I trust you are having in this moment: Snow and blowing snow in December in Wisconsin!

In fact, when I asked, they trusted a very positive response was shared, *Gentle winter so far, minimal winds and only about five to six inches of fresh snow each day.*

Five to six inches a day was minor for them but, since I was in San Diego, California with the most days at 72 degrees (confirmed in the encyclopedia) … I hesitated but, God confirmed I was going to go and my flight was already scheduled for the next morning.

The man I met with was immediately intrigued by my story about the government actions while the Superior Court Judges and trial attorneys were being investigated before a few were sentenced to Federal prison on RICO (racketeering) charges. During the investigation phase, agents were requiring multiple ID changes at the same time as the additional crime of ID theft was emerging, before it was understood or addressed as a crime. The man was intrigued by 'my story', a story outlined within a script which won a film festival competition due to being 'a compelling story'.

Shortly after we met, God arranged for him to go south for the winter. He stopped in Savannah, Georgia. He met a well known former Hollywood film producer and three of the lead actors from his films. When he returned to Wisconsin in April 2013, God prompted him to call me and arrange an introduction for me with the Savannah based film producer.

My first reaction was laughter.

Why? The producer became well known in Hollywood but, he is not in Los Angeles. He has relocated to Savannah, Georgia.

Truth: Savannah is on the complete opposite side of the country from Hollywood producers in Los Angeles, a reasonable drive from my home in San Diego. However, God prompted me to pray about the details because <u>God orchestrated this connection</u>.

Within days, our Father arranged a few confirmations from completely different resources about the exact same fact: *More films are being produced in Georgia than in Hollywood.*

Within three months, God arranged for me to be in Georgia for three days. I was in Macon, about two or three hours West of Savannah. Within six months of the call, our Father placed my feet in Savannah, Georgia. Plus, God arranged for me to meet the film producer. God arranged for the man to be available the moment I arrived at his office and we actually met twice within 24 hours. Meetings were held during the first two days of my three week trip and they were very productive.

Since October 2013, I have remained in Georgia even though God initially confirmed the exact dates of ONLY three weeks.

Now, nearly five years later, the timing for the film is close at hand. Hopefully, the timing will result in another example of what people often find out is a 15-20 year 'overnight success' story!

GOD drew my attention to Savannah for an additional purpose, also, a purpose he disclosed during a conversation with Heather Rock during the development of *For The Sake Of America II*. He also confirmed the fact within the Apocrypha:

The Second Book of Esdras, 13:29+ (emphasis added)
Explanation of vision given to Ezra.
Verse 29+. Behold, the days are coming when the Most High is going to deliver those who are on the earth, and amazement will come upon those who live on the earth, and they will plan to make war one upon another, city upon city and place upon place, people upon people, and kingdom upon kingdom.

32 And it will come about, when this happens that the signs will occur which I showed you before, and my Son will be revealed, whom you saw as a man coming up.

33 And it will come about, when all the nations hear his voice, that every man will leave his country and the wars that they have with one another, and a countless multitude such as you saw will be gathered together, wishing to come and subdue him. But he will stand on the top of Mount Zion. And Zion will come and be revealed to all men, made ready and built like the mountain that you saw carved out without hands.

37 And my Son will charge the heathen who have come with their ungodliness (this was symbolized by the storm), and will upbraid them to their face with their evil thoughts and the tortures with which they are to be tortured (which were symbolized by the flame), and he will destroy them without effort by the Law (which is symbolized by the fire).

39 And as for seeing him gather about himself another multitude that was peaceable, **these are the ten tribes that in the days of King Hoshea were carried away from their own land into captivity, whom Shalmaneser, king of Assyria, made captives, and carried beyond the river; they were carried off to another country. <u>But</u> they formed this plan among themselves, to leave the heathen population, and go to a more distant region, where the human race had never lived, so that there perhaps they might keep their statutes, which they had not kept in their own country. And <u>they went in by the narrow passages</u> of the Euphrates River. For the Most High then did wonders for them, for he held back the sources of the river**

until they had passed over. But it was a long journey of a year and a half to that country, and the country is called Azaerath.

46 There they have lived until the last time, and now, when they are about to come again, the Most High will hold back the sources of the river again, so that they can cross over, It is on that account that you saw the multitude gathered together in peace. But those also who are left of your people, who are found within my holy borders, will live. Therefore it will be that when he destroys the multitude of the nations that are gathered together, he will protect the people that remain, and then he will show them many, many wonders.

When we review the original information from the Apocrypha, which states the LORD took up the water and the people walked for a year and a half, it seemed impossible to imagine the people would arrive on the East Coast of America.

Research confirmed the people traveling in about 500 BC were walking a shorter distance with America being referred to as 'across the pond' from England for centuries. The 'across the pond' is still used as of today!

Finally, after multiple promptings from our Father to research the facts, I looked at the maps and 'in current day' mileage, the distance from the mouth of the Euphrates River to the Savannah, Georgia port is 6940 miles. Yikes! That is a long way to walk!

In the midst of thinking that walk would be absolutely impossible, God said, again, *Through Me all things are possible.*

So, I researched the facts again. Truth is truth!

The truth of this matter is confirmed with a 3000 mile journey being completed easily within six months. To be sure, I researched for a 'second opinion' and a man actually chose to walk across the nation from the far Northeast to the far Southwest of America. He toured interesting locations along the way while completing the trip in less than six months. Therefore, it appears 6940 within 18 months is absolutely possible.

Why did the LORD prompt me to research the route from the Euphrates River mouth to Savannah, Georgia?

Well, I trust you know me well enough by now to realize I questioned this request immediately!

This portion of the research was grueling because I am not from Georgia and even though our Father has focused me for so long upon uncovering and revealing so many lies and evil roots established in Georgia, this request was unique.

Continuing to seek the truth because God knows we must repent to heal our land.

Yes. The land God is referring to actually starts with each of us, individually, repenting on behalf of our own hunk of dust!

It is clear to all current citizens of America that families have traveled across America exactly as the Native Americans were located on the land from the East to the West Coast, and beyond.

God confirmed the truth was already available.

This was puzzling.

While I prayed, God confirmed I need to research the location of the Euphrates River mouth and the Savannah, Georgia port.

WOW!

Heather Rock mentioned the potential of this during a prior conversation, and yet, this information is so far beyond my level of knowledge or understanding I did nor proceed to research the facts.

However, while I was in a conversation with a prayer partner and intercessor for my ministry our LORD confirmed the truth and within hours, He revealed the same truth is confirmed on some bible maps:

Euphrates River mouth location: 32 degrees North.

Savannah, Georgia port location: 32 degrees North.

God provided even more specifics while I was lining up the two latitude facts. Originally, I typed Mouth of Euphrates River and it made the line much longer so I was praying about the spacing issue so I could have the two answers line up. God prompted me to change how I worded the line and then – like a miracle – the two lines were perfectly aligned!

More proof of what our Father shared above, and within *For The Sake Of America II.*

The Apocrypha described the facts of taking up the water for the tribes to walk for 18 months. Not all people walked for 18 months since some have shown up in Spain, the islands and other nations.

However, it is exciting to see the latitude facts since latitude lines were unknown for centuries after the lost tribes of Israel journeyed for 18 months and yet, the truth is exciting since it confirms the truth within the Apocrypha which was included in the 1611 bible remains 'in tact' from about 500 BC to the current day.

How is 32 degrees North important in current times?

Where is the 32 degrees North located within Iraq?

Al Hillah, the Crescent.

Al Hillah is the capital of Babil or Babel.

When the Iraq war began, the first Marines landing on the soil were immediately sent to protect Hillah or Hilla, the capital of Babylon. Why?

What did Native Indians know without 'a bible in hand'?

The Native Indians knew the history of the region, the building of a tower of Babel, known as a tower being built to the sky.

Native Indians survived the many divisions of the tribes.

The naming of many other Indian tribes within America alone confirms division of the family existed among the original families of the twelve sons and therefore the tribes of Jacob/Israel were dividing exactly as the denominations have repeatedly divided the believers to this day.

Sad status to realize how often divisions are happening among believers.

We have evidently not realized the simple plan of the enemy to divide and conquer.

It is our shift. *LORD help us wake up believers to Your truth!*

Lesson: The Native Indians were removed 'from their homes and land' by the new arrivals to the land within about 50 years after America became a new nation.

Within 200 years of the Native Indian Removal Act, there are so many arrivals upon our land our laws are being challenged for us to remain in our homes and retain our land, our freedom and our liberty.

Clearly, God orchestrated and guided the journey of the tribes!

Plus, He has promised to take up the water once again for the return of the tribes!

When God arranges for the return will we be His people, known by His name, included in the multitude gathered together with our Father?

Will we be known as GOD's people?

II Chronicles 7:14. *If My people who are called by My name will humble themselves, and pray and seek My face, and turn from their wicked ways* (REPENT), *then I will hear from heaven, and will forgive their sin and heal their land* (RESTORE).

Will we repent for all that is known and what is unknown in this hour? **Praying we will repent for ALL our Father reveals!**

Chapter 6   Tribes of Israel, Significance to America

Twelve tribes in Israel, the twelve sons of Jacob / Israel.

Ten tribes in the north joined together in 930 BC and they were known as the Kingdom of Israel (some Indian tribes identified):

Reuben	**Seminole and Muskogee +**
Simeon	**Found in America & other nations, also**
Dan	**Found in Amerixa & other nations, also**
Naphtali	**Found in island & other nations, also**
Gad	**Combination of Native American Tribes**
Asher	**Chocktaw? Found in island nations, also**
Issachar	**Cherokee, perhaps Blackfoot & Iroquois**
Zebulon	**Cheyenne? Apache? Osage & Ute?**
Manasseh	**Creek / Muskogee**
Ephraim	**Chippewa**

Over the centuries, divisions have taken place.

Several people notified me of their Indian lineage after the release of *For The Sake Of America II.* Many are still in the Southeast who are linked to Cherokee and Creek, and some are Blackfoot, Chocktaw & Chippewa, etc. Some also know the tribe they represent based upon the truth told by elders generation to generation.

The maps of the tribes are 'as good as the person preparing the maps'. Plus, due to the continued divisions among the tribes it is not easy to limit the Native Indian tribes. Also, marriages between the tribes over the centuries result in multiple tribes often being represented within the family vs. being from a single Native tribe or one tribe of Israel. Few facts are published for the smaller tribes.

The additional two tribes remained together in the South and they became the Kingdom of Judah:

Judah

Benjamin

Some of the people have identified being from the tribes of Israel, while the family lineage is from Benjamin.

Blessings spoken over the sons of Jacob / Israel, by Jacob:

Genesis 49. Jacob's Last Words to His Sons.

And Jacob called his sons and said, *"Gather together, that I may tell you what shall befall you in the last days:*

2 "Gather together and hear, you sons of Jacob,

And listen to Israel your father.

3 *"Reuben, you are my firstborn,*
   My might and the beginning of my strength,
   The excellency of dignity and the excellency of power.

4 *Unstable as water, you shall not excel,*
   Because you went up to your father's bed;
   Then you defiled it—
   He went up to my couch.

5 *"Simeon and Levi are brothers;*
   Instruments of cruelty are in their dwelling place.

6 *Let not my soul enter their council;*
   Let not my honor be united to their assembly;
   For in their anger they slew a man,
   And in their self-will they hamstrung an ox.

7 *Cursed be their anger, for it is fierce;*
   And their wrath, for it is cruel!
   I will divide them in Jacob
   And scatter them in Israel.

8 *"Judah, you are he whom your brothers shall praise;*
   Your hand shall be on the neck of your enemies;
   Your father's children shall bow down before you.

9 *Judah is a lion's whelp;*
   From the prey, my son, you have gone up.
   He bows down, he lies down as a lion;
   And as a lion, who shall rouse him?

10 *The scepter shall not depart from Judah,*
    Nor a lawgiver from between his feet,

Until Shiloh comes;
And to Him shall be the obedience of the people.

11 *Binding his donkey to the vine,*
   And his donkey's colt to the choice vine,
   He washed his garments in wine,
   And his clothes in the blood of grapes.

12 *His eyes are darker than wine,*
   And his teeth whiter than milk.

13 *"Zebulun shall dwell by the haven of the sea;*
   He shall become a haven for ships,
   And his border shall adjoin Sidon.

14 *"Issachar is a strong donkey,*
   Lying down between two burdens;

15 *He saw that rest was good,*
   And that the land was pleasant;
   He bowed his shoulder to bear a burden,
   And became a band of slaves.

16 *"Dan shall judge his people*
   As one of the tribes of Israel.

17 *Dan shall be a serpent by the way,*
   A viper by the path,
   That bites the horse's heels
   So that its rider shall fall backward.

18 *I have waited for your salvation, O LORD!*

19 *"Gad, a troop shall tramp upon him,*
   But he shall triumph at last.

20 *"Bread from Asher shall be rich,*
   And he shall yield royal dainties.

21 *"Naphtali is a deer let loose;*
   He uses beautiful words.

22 *"Joseph is a fruitful bough,*
   A fruitful bough by a well;
   His branches run over the wall.

23 *The archers have bitterly grieved him,*
   Shot at him and hated him.

24 *But his bow remained in strength,*
   And the arms of his hands were made strong
   By the hands of the Mighty God of Jacob
   (From there is the Shepherd, the Stone of Israel),

25 *By the God of your father who will help you,*
   And by the Almighty who will bless you
   With blessings of heaven above,
   Blessings of the deep that lies beneath,
   Blessings of the breasts and of the womb.

26 *The blessings of your father*
   Have excelled the blessings of my ancestors,
   Up to the utmost bound of the everlasting hills.
   They shall be on the head of Joseph,
   And on the crown of the head of him who was separate
   from his brothers.

27 *"Benjamin is a ravenous wolf;*
   In the morning he shall devour the prey,
   And at night he shall divide the spoil."

28 *All these are the twelve tribes of Israel, and this is what*
their father spoke to them. And he blessed them; he blessed each
one according to his own blessing.

Truth per Ancient Map and within the Apocrypha:

The King of Assyria took the ten tribes in the north captive in 721 BC according to the ancient map by Adams.

The comment on the Ancient chronological map:

Never to return.

THE END OF ISRAEL.

The ten tribes, Kingdom of Israel, became known as the *"Lost Tribes of Israel"* when they departed for the new, uninhabited land by about 500 BC.

Since they are all 'sons of Jacob/Israel' did they all journey at the same time? 500 BC is identified as the date due to the Cherokee artifact of the Ten Commandments etched on stone in Paleo Hebrew of about 500 BC.

The answer for all of the tribes?

This is a guess due to minimal records.

Artifacts 'etched in stone' are dated as 10th century BC, also.

Gold artifacts from Solomon's temple and ancient Israel are 'beyond our comprehension'. They are on the land in America, also.

People have contacted me with great emotion while confirming they are members of each tribe of Israel. They were Native American Indians who are being called 'African Americans' now. They have the documents and they know they are members of the tribes. Members of the tribes of Judah and Benjamin also consider themselves as the tribes of Israel and state they are merely from the South Israel region. They are also represented 'on the land' in

118

America in these days. Families have documents which confirm their lineage going back many, many generations.

Confusion did not enter family history until the Removal Act.

Wondering: Did the ten tribes depart for the new, uninhabited land alone or did our Father orchestrate their travel by taking up all of the water and guiding them together with the Kingdom of Judah during the 18 month journey?

Or, did the tribes in the south proceed to Spain and arrive with Christopher Columbus in 1492? Or ...

As soon as *For The Sake Of America II* was released, people told me which tribe their family was linked to and their family status caused me to do even more research because they identified both the tribes within the Kingdom of Israel and Judah.

Wondering: Did all of the members of the tribes come to the new, uninhabited land which later became America? NO.

Some are in other nations around the world.

In America, many of the tribes knew the Cherokee preserved the creator's name and the spellings vary while the many versions are clearly versions of Yahweh. Many knew the Cherokee were leaders and fought for their rights, freedom and liberty.

Due to the lack of communication options to share information region to region across the nation, the location of the Native Indians in the south, especially Georgia to North Carolina became the focus for the Native Indian Removal Act.

Remember, our Father positioned the angelic vortexes at Macon, Georgia and Moravian Falls, North Carolina.

The status was evidently not realized by the other tribes 'in the West' because they were unaware and they were not 'immediately affected'. Their notification appears to have taken place when new settlers were arriving in their regions. With little or no notice, their homes, their land, their rights, freedom and liberty were removed.

It was easier for the push out of homes and off their land to proceed because the tribes were divided so many times before the 'new settlers' arrived. Therefore, they were not united together to deal with what was happening from tribe to tribe, nation to nation, territory to territory in any of the regions across the land.

While they were still united, the elders repeated the stories generation to generation.

Members of the original tribes have heard and continue to share the stories which were specific to the facts shared generation to generation for more than 2300 years! Then, within a few years of 'new settlers' changing everything about the agreements for the land. Everything changed faster than the Native Indians could comprehend or react.

Missionaries & ministers who knew the truth about the Native Indians fought with them and on their behalf. Many who tried to counter the invasion resulting in the Native Indian Removal Act were sentenced to prison terms and they served in labor camps.

LORD reveal to us what we need to repent for now and help us unite together in Your truth as fellow believers! Help us do everything we can so it will become on earth as it is in heaven for there are no divisions, no denominations, no separations or sectarianism which You have confirmed as sin, in heaven.

<u>A few examples</u>: **Cherokee warriors** were known as the tribe who carried the ark into battle. They maintained the Hebrew seven feasts and festivals and honored the Sabbath or seventh day rest. They chose to not eat pork and they provided cities of refuge. They are recognized as the Tribe of **Issachar.**

NOTE: Iroquois tribe is often aligned with Cherokee.

Chocktaw held to the exact same beliefs. They also passed down the story when the world was all land until the Creator visited Nuah, told him to build a raft to save mankind when the world was covered with water. They also know that the earth was originally provided as the land for all, one nation, united.

Chocktaw also knew mankind tried to build a sky tower, the tower of Babel. They knew it was only the Creator in the sky. Trusting they were doing all they could to understand our portals between earth and heaven.

Many scriptures cover this topic of portals between earth and heaven. A good resource which confirms these facts is: ***Portals of Heaven*** book and CD series by Rebecca King. Her Sid Roth radio and TV interviews can be found within the archives. The radio interview aired during March 2015 and the TV interview aired during the week of April 20, 2015.

Chippewa know they are known as the people of the prophet, Anshe Navi in Hebrew and recognized as the Tribe of **Ephriam.**

Tribes resemble the church today:

Many tribes! Many divisions!

Growing up in the Midwest, in Nebraska, it was obvious that the people have a deep belief in the Great Spirit, the Creator. It was evident among the Pawnee, Ponca, Sioux, Navajo, Lakota, etc.

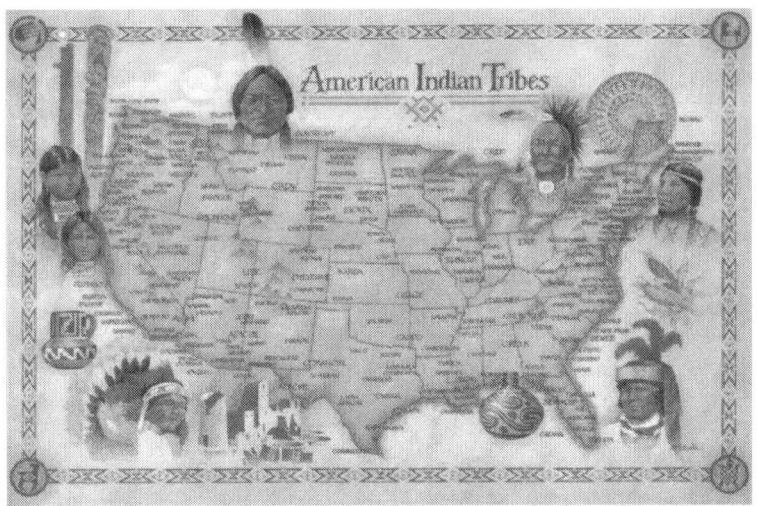

Maps vary; Map shared from Legends of America website.

Many divisions among the original tribes of Israel and the Native tribes across America. However, we need to remember that our LORD sent the tribes of Israel to the 'uninhabited land' more than 2000 years ago! The expansion of the church did not take place until 1500 AD!

Much for us to repent for and pray about so we will know all our Father is wanting us to be aware of for we each have a purpose and plan to fulfill upon while we are representing our Father as Ambassadors for Christ while we are living on earth, doing all we can so it will become on Earth as it is in Heaven!

Chapter 7   Choice of Believers, Significance to America

We are at choice: *As Elijah confirmed we have a choice to make regarding who we will serve, either Baal or the only living LORD.*

The choice remains the same today!

When God prompts me to meet with a pastor or ministry leader, He often directs me to hold the salt and pepper shakers. When His time is right during the meeting, he asks me to demonstrate the truth He has revealed to me. The choice is this simple: Salt shaker, Kingdom of Heaven; Pepper shaker, Kingdom on Earth, the World.

When we speak, which Kingdom do we represent?

When we offer assistance, which Kingdom do we represent?

When we negotiate a matter, which Kingdom do we represent?

The questions help us see our choices!

We either represent the only living LORD, or we do not!

We have leaned on our own understanding so much 'over time', the review of the 2016 election stated 40% of the pastors across America were not sure who they were going to vote for as of the week of the election!

Choosing to listen to our Father or opinions of man?

LORD forgive us!

LORD we thank You for keeping Your hand upon us and blessing this nation! Thank You for remaining with us and guiding us in our choices in these days!

Always Speak Life became a separate book due to what I was hearing from men and women who have been 'in the church' for decades and some for all of their days but, they did not realize we have LIFE with Christ on earth and in heaven so we should *Always Speak Life.*

Truth:

Our words are our HIStory to all who have ears to hear.

We are speaking life or death!

We are speaking truth or lies!

We are speaking blessings or curses!

We are expressing who we are serving!

We are at choice! Which Kingdom do we represent?

Repeating lies by sharing what 'other people said' is often merely gossip or lies. We need to research for facts, know the truth before we speak forth any words to others!

We are at choice regarding the words coming from our lips!

What we say reveals who we represent, LORD or not!

Yes. We either represent the only living LORD or the enemy.

Who do we listen to? Who will we follow?

What is our choice between the two: LORD or Baal (gods).

Will we stand firm in truth? Or, will we back away in fear and help hide believers and representatives of the only living LORD as Obadiah did until God sent Elijah? Praying we will stand firm in the truth, in faith and believe our GOD is the only living LORD and the command we will accept. Choose!

We have divided so many times 'as a people' and used our words pointing out stacks of differences in 'thinking or theology' by often following man's interpretation and we may have used it as the reason to judge and separate from people vs. seeking GOD's truth before we proceed.

Important to realize the ONLY truth is we were each made in God's image and He made each of us as part of a holy nation, a peculiar people: **I Peter 2:9-10.** *But you are a chosen generation, a royal priesthood, a holy nation, His own special people, that you may proclaim the praises of Him who called you out of darkness into His marvelous light;* **10** *who once were not a* *people but are now the people of God, who had not obtained mercy but now have obtained mercy.*

Do we appreciate being peculiar? Do we really know who we are? Do we truly know which family are we grafted into?

If we were asked in this moment 'whom do you choose to serve' would we be able to share the truth without an ounce of hesitation? Would we easily confirm we are in the family of the only living LORD, joint heir with Christ, a son/daughter of the most High God?

Living Before the World.
I Peter 2:11-12. *Beloved, I beg you as sojourners and pilgrims, abstain from fleshly lusts which war against the soul,* **12** *having your conduct honorable among the Gentiles, that when they speak against you as evildoers, they may, by your good works which they observe, <u>glorify God in the day of visitation</u>.*

Our choice is evident in our actions and our words even if we think we may not have chosen who we will follow. Others hear it and see it, even if we are not realizing it is evident. How we make choices on a daily basis confirms who we are aligned with, as Elijah confirmed the choice: *If the LORD is* (your) *God, follow Him; but if Baal, follow him."*

I Kings 18: 20-21.
Elijah's Mount Carmel Victory.
So Ahab sent for all the children of Israel, and gathered the prophets together on Mount Carmel. **21** And Elijah came to all the

people, and said, *"How long will you falter between two opinions? If the Lord is God, follow Him; but if Baal, follow him."* But the people answered him not a word.

Obadiah hid prophets of the LORD.

Obadiah was in fear of King Ahab when Elijah approached him and told him to inform the King that Elijah was bringing rain!

Elijah told Obadiah to gather the prophets for Baal.

They all gathered and became witnesses to the truth, what the only living LORD is capable of doing while none of the Baals were able to do anything, and what our only living LORD would do for the people in bringing rain to end the drought after the people acknowledged God's prophet Elijah truly represented the only living LORD who heard the people and answered their prayer.

I Kings 18: 22+.

Then Elijah said to the people, *"I alone am left a prophet of the Lord; but Baal's prophets are four hundred and fifty men. 23 Therefore let them give us two bulls; and let them choose one bull for themselves, cut it in pieces, and lay it on the wood, but put no fire under it; and I will prepare the other bull, and lay it on the wood, but put no fire under it. 24 Then you call on the name of your gods, and I will call on the name of the Lord; and the God who answers by fire, He is God."*

So all the people answered and said, *"It is well spoken."*

Knowing the truth and standing firm in faith, believing in the only living LORD and acting upon the truth is a separate choice.

I Kings 18: 25+. (Faith being put into action.)

Now Elijah said to the prophets of Baal, *"Choose one bull for yourselves and prepare it first, for you are many; and call on the name of your god, but put no fire under it."*

26 So they took the bull which was given them, and they prepared *it,* and called on the name of Baal from morning even till noon, saying, *"O Baal, hear us!"* But *there was* no voice; no one answered. Then they leaped about the altar which they had made.

27 And so it was, at noon, that Elijah mocked them and said, *"Cry aloud, for he is a god; either he is meditating, or he is busy, or he is on a journey, or perhaps he is sleeping and must be awakened."*

28 So they cried aloud, and cut themselves, as was their custom, with knives and lances, until the blood gushed out on them. 29 And when midday was past, they prophesied until the *time* of the offering of the *evening* sacrifice. But *there was* no voice; no one answered, no one paid attention.

30 Then Elijah said to all the people, *"Come near to me."* So all the people came near to him. And he repaired the altar of the Lord *that was* broken down. 31 And Elijah took twelve stones, according to the number of the tribes of the sons of Jacob, to whom the word of the Lord had come, saying, *"Israel shall be your name."*

32 Then with the stones he built an altar in the name of the Lord; and he made a trench around the altar large enough to hold two seahs of seed.

33 And he put the wood in order, cut the bull in pieces, and laid *it* on the wood, and said, *"Fill four water pots with water, and pour it on the burnt sacrifice and on the wood."*

34 Then he said, *"Do it a second time,"* and they did *it* a second time; and he said, *"Do it a third time,"* and they did *it* a third time.

35 So the water ran all around the altar; and he also filled the trench with water.

36 And it came to pass, at *the time of* the offering of the *evening* sacrifice, that Elijah the prophet came near and said, *"Lord God of Abraham, Isaac, and Israel, let it be known this day that You are God in Israel and I am Your servant, and that I have done all these things at Your word. 37 Hear me, O Lord, hear me, that this people may know that You are the Lord God, and that You have turned their hearts back to You again."*

38 Then the fire of the Lord fell and consumed the burnt sacrifice, and the wood and the stones and the dust, and it licked up the water that *was* in the trench. **39** Now when all the people saw *it,* they fell on their faces; and they said, *"The Lord, He is God! The Lord, He is God!"*

I Kings 18: 40. (Consequences)

40 And Elijah said to them, *"Seize the prophets of Baal! Do not let one of them escape!"* So they seized them; and Elijah brought them down to the Brook Kishon and executed them there.

The Drought Ends

41 Then Elijah said to Ahab, *"Go up, eat and drink; for there is the sound of abundance of rain."* **42** So Ahab went up to eat and drink. And Elijah went up to the top of Carmel; then he bowed down on the ground, and put his face between his knees, **43** and said to his servant, *"Go up now, look toward the sea."*

So he went up and looked, and said, *"There is nothing."* And seven times he said, *"Go again."*

44 Then it came to pass the seventh *time,* that he said, *"There is a cloud, as small as a man's hand, rising out of the sea!"* So he said, *"Go up, say to Ahab, 'Prepare your chariot, and go down before the rain stops you.'"*

45 Now it happened in the meantime that the sky became black with clouds and wind, and there was a heavy rain. So Ahab rode away and went to Jezreel. **46** Then the hand of the Lord came upon Elijah; and he girded up his loins and ran ahead of Ahab to the entrance of Jezreel.

GOD transported His victor, Elijah, so he would arrive before Ahab arrived within his chariot!

Drought ends in 2018!

Special miracle in 2018!

Drought ends in Capetown, South Africa.

Pastor Rodney Howard-Browne heard about the 'last day of water deadline' in Capetown due to the drought they experienced.

GOD prompted Pastor Rodney and Adonica Browne to go and share the gospel, hold a crusade, declare the truth about the only living LORD.

Results? More than 5,000 salvations!

Rain filled the dams, rivers and lakes.

The drought ended!

Fabulous video summary is available on The River at Tampa Bay Church ministry website: revival.com.

Even Adam had a choice to make after his sin was revealed to him. GOD spoke it in clear terms to Adan but, it was ignored by Adam.

Genesis 3:22-24.

Then the Lord God said, *"Behold, the man has become like one of Us, to know good and evil. And now, <u>lest he put out his hand and take also of the tree of life, and eat, and live forever"</u>*—

PAUSE. It is time to choose the only living LORD!
God provided a pause after He declared the truth.
Right now, as a body of believers, our GOD has allowed a PAUSE for us after He has declared the truth.
His desire is for us to hear the truth!
Then, GOD will proceed exactly as He did with Adam.

23 therefore the Lord God sent him out of the garden of Eden to till the ground from which he was taken. **24** So He drove out the man; and He placed cherubim at the east of the garden of Eden, **<u>and a flaming sword which turned every way, to guard the way to the tree of life.</u>**

God spoke to Adam, giving him another option to **choose life**!

The cherubim at the gate to the garden **turned their sword every way, <u>to guard the way to the tree of life.</u>**

What did Adam do? Adam was silent. Then, Adam departed.

LORD help us wake up to your truth and **choose life!**

Even **Noah** had another choice he could make, day after day after day for more than 100 years of being a pastor, he still chose the truth. Noah still chose LIFE!

131

Noah confirmed by his actions: *For me and my family will serve the only living LORD!*

Wow. For more than 100 years, Noah stood firm in truth and shared the truth even though everyone he knew in the world beyond Methuselah (his grandfather) spoke against him.

Noah did not depart from the truth. Truth was his choice.

Noah personally chose to follow the instructions of our LORD.

In the face of more than 100 years of ridicule, Noah did not depart from the plans God gave him to build the ark and share a very important message for the people to trust the rain (which did not come from heaven in the past) would come from above and flood the earth so it was time to choose who they would serve, Baal (gods) or the only living LORD.

The choice is still the same for us today!

Whatever we are putting up with, it is rare to deal with ANYTHING for a period of time even close to 100 years!

What is our choice as we enter into each new day?

What is our choice when we are in conversation with others?

Who are we choosing to represent?

Who are we choosing to stand firm with when we are in the marketplace, in the community?

Do we have what it takes to stand firm in the truth with our Father, to live an abundant life and prosper while being ridiculed for more than 100 years?

Our choice is evident to all who have eyes to see and ears to hear. Now that we realize we are at choice, I pray every word we share and every action we take reflects that we know what we are saying and we are choosing to represent the only living LORD!

America was a blessed nation which grew into 'One Nation Under GOD' and we had every opportunity to live in freedom and liberty by receiving the truth through the Native Americans, then, the Pilgrims.

Everything was at peace for centuries!

Since those days we have operated exactly as the oppressors of ancient times, ancient kingdoms, ancient structure of the Pharisees by becoming judges of others and not loving those made in Your image! Forgive us LORD!

We have become a people which are not easy to recognize in the world as believers because we have become compromised with the world and therefore, too much like the world for the non-believers to see a difference! Forgive us LORD!

We have not sought the truth from You, from the bible, so we have become so worldly to focus upon the competition to become successful in the world that it is showing up everywhere, in everything, in every area of our lives, between siblings and between spouses, between children and parents and it has allowed the access of evil motives to enter into the hearts of even those who profess to know You and serve You. Forgive us LORD!

LORD, forgive us and help us while we open our hearts and minds anew to Your deeper truth being revealed, to allow Christ to reside deep in our hearts and renew the resurrection power in us, while we become aligned with Your will so our minds will become conformed to the mind of Christ!

LORD reveal ALL to us in these days so we can fully serve You and share the truth to the four corners of the earth for You are the truth!

II Chronicles 7:14. *If My people who are called by My name will humble themselves, and pray and seek My face, and turn from their wicked ways* (**REPENT**), *then I will hear from heaven, and will forgive their sin and heal their land* (**RESTORE**).

Choose Liberty & Freedom, *For The Sake Of America!*

May the truth shared within these pages bless you, fill you to overflowing, and cause you to share it with all members of your family, extended family, all friends, fellow believers, and those who seek the truth and want a relationship with the only living LORD, the Father, the Son and the Holy Spirit.

May all in your household, family and extended family, be able to declare: as for me and my house, we will serve the LORD!

LORD we are grateful that You have given us Your truth in Your Word. We are thankful You reveal it to us, for we do know You sent Your Son to us 'in the world' as our Savior, our Prince of Peace, the Word, the Way, the Truth and the Light.

Proverbs 22:6.

Train up a child in the way he should go,

And when he is old he will not depart from it.

II Chronicles 7:14. *if My people who are called by My name will humble themselves, and pray and seek My face, and turn from their wicked ways (REPENT), then I will hear from heaven, and will forgive their sin and heal their land (RESTORE).*

Praying We The People will gather together NOW as a body of believers with full faith and pray specifically for GOD's divine protection for America, for our President and for ALL in leadership who are operating in truth! May all be revealed to us which is NOT truth so ALL who are given the leadership opportunity will seek truth and serve the people in truth!

AMEN ... OUR GOD IS A FAITHFUL KING!

REVIEW   God's Plan Reviewed, Significance to America

Acts 5:38. *And now I say to you, keep away from these men and let them alone; for if this plan or this work is of men, it will come to nothing 39 but if it is of God, you cannot overthrow it – lest you even be found to fight against God.*

500 year plan. The Pilgrims established a 500 year plan.

IF the plan began upon arrival in 1620, the plan would proceed with all 'living free, in peace on the land' until 2120.

They followed God's plan to live in liberty and freedom for 500 years. We did not remain aligned with the plan for 200 years!

America is not 'in trouble' due to a couple of political decisions such as the previous administration or the removal of prayer from public schools. We allowed change. We aligned with other choices!

The Tribes of Israel, the sons of Jacob / Israel, had a choice to make, to either remain enslaved in Assyria or proceed to the uninhabited land GOD provided.

They followed the plan of our Father, the Creator.

They walked for 18 months, guided by our Father.

The tribes remained 'in peace', governed by Divine Law, living on the land of abundance GOD provided from about 500 (or 600) BC until the 1800's! They arrived and were living on the land 2000 years before it became America, a time period within the stone age.

What did they etch on stone?

The Ten Commandments & Praise be to Yah!

Ark of the Covenant carried into Battle!

The Seven Feasts & Festivals Honored!

This is why our history is recorded by them in ancient Paleo Hebrew upon stone, exactly as we found with the Ten Commandments and a 10th century BC artifact preserved and donated to the Cherokee Museum in Cherokee, North Carolina.

These artifacts confirm the Hebrew language was preserved from the ancient Paleo Hebrew whether they were brought to America by the 'Lost Tribes of Israel' or they were prepared by them once they arrived.

500-600 BC to 1800 AD.

Peace was retained in a land not called America until 1492.

From the Stone Age to Modern History (started in 1453), peace was preserved on the land named America by Columbus in 1492.

What was happening globally?

1455 Pope confirmed reading first printed bible; small part of the current bible as the New Testament was not added until 1500's.

1492 Columbus arrived with the exiled Jews who escaped from Spain. Jews had experienced severe persecution from Spain before they journeyed to the new land. Dark Ages / Middle Ages, a time period which began in the fifth century AD with the collapse of the Roman Empire and continued until 1453, transitioned to the current time period referred to as Modern History.

1517 Martin Luther posted the 95 theses; bible still in German. Martin Luther posted the theses based upon his anger with Pope Leo X's new round of 'indulgences' (good words or payments to cancel out sins; described by Luther as corrupting people's faith) to help build St. Peter's Basilica.

Luther hoped the points would lead to an open discussion. Copies spread throughout the region within two weeks, throughout Europe within two months. Results: Luther was excommunicated from the Catholic Church.

1535 William Tyndale translated the bible direct from Hebrew and Greek texts. Published copies were smuggled into England by merchants. **(DVD: *God's Outlaw*,** Tyndale's life story)

Pilgrims / Puritans taught their children the Lord's Prayer and scriptures in English.

1536 King Henry VIII was counseled that the people would become independent of the monarchy if the bible became available in English. People were imprisoned and burned at the stake for possessing a bible or speaking scriptures in English, including the martyrs involved with Tyndale and then, Tyndale in 1536.

King Henry VIII approved a bible for distribution within three years of executing Tyndale, in 1539.

1539 bible version includes most of the Tyndale bible translation while all credit was given to Myles Coverdale.

1611 King James bible was distributed.

This version included the Apocrypha.

Apocrypha remained until 1835 when it was removed by the British and Foreign Bible Society. The society was formed in 1804.

Coincidence?

Life changed for the 'Lost Tribes of Israel', the Native American Indians in 1804, also. Treaty signings were frequent with the transfer of significant parcels of land to the 'new government'. The Native Americans knew no deeds were to be in 'human names' because all of the land belongs to our Father.

Native Indian Removal Act in 1830; forced to leave their homes and land (1831-1850) even though the Cherokee won their case in the Supreme Court.

Shortly after the Native American Indians were removed from their homes and their land through the Indian Removal Act in 1830, two years after gold was discovered in Georgia, 1828, the British and Foreign Bible Society removed the Apocrypha in 1835!

Coincidence?

People in England were still being imprisoned and burned at the stake for studying the English bible, meeting in groups separate from the Church of England. Residents were still being forced to attend the Church of England.

People were not allowed to miss services of the Church of England (formerly the Catholic Church until King Henry required changes to marry and divorce to marry who he wanted to marry).

In fact, when Puritans (purely follow the bible 'as is') were found in homes or public locations sharing the bible and meeting to fellowship, they were arrested and imprisoned. This status continued even after Pilgrims/Puritans left England the first time. They were imprisoned before their second departure.

1604 Pilgrims began their plan to depart from England. The journey is traced within a DVD by Kirk Cameron, *Monumental.*

1620 Pilgrims arrive at Plymouth Rock.

Pilgrims made a choice to sacrifice everything, including their assets, their friends, family and even their life, with nearly half of the Pilgrims dying during the first winter before they joined the inhabitants on the new land known as America.

Pilgrims lived 'in peace' with the Native Indians and the Jews from Spain. How? They were able to 'live in peace', aligned together in the 'same truth' with the 500 year plan established to live in and retain liberty and freedom for the current & future generations.

They remained in peace with the Indians and Jews 'on the land' and operated in truth, sharing from the LORD's abundance of provision. Native Indians shared everything with the Jews when they arrived from Spain in 1492, and again when the Pilgrims arrived in 1620 AD.

Native Indians retained peace together through the arrival of Europeans in greater and greater numbers in the 1700's, after living free on the land for about 2300 years. They knew and lived according to GOD's Divine Law. They knew GOD's provision would be 'more than enough' during the establishment of the Colonies until 1732 when Georgia was structured as the last colony in 1732.

Native Indians lived in peace and shared the abundance from the land for more than 2000 years before the Jews arrived and for more than 100 years before the Pilgrims arrived because they knew their Creator and the Great Spirit. They passed on the truth about GOD's provision and how the people 'in the bible' lived without having a 'printed bible' to refer to! Wow! 2300 years of retaining peace and sharing truth changed within less 100 years! In fact, in less than 60 years.

By 1830, an American law was passed, a Native Indian Removal Act. The very people who inhabited the land for 2300 years were removed in less than 100 years from the Colonies being fully established with their help.

Within 50 years after they participated in the battles to help America become an independent nation, they were ordered to leave their homes and land. What a bizarre "Jubilee" (50 year increment) for them!

Pattern of 'what happened' to America after Native Indians were living in truth and peace on the land for more than 2000 years is briefly summarized as follows:

100 Years
1500-1600

1492 – 1604 / 1620

Jews from Spain arrived. They escaped persecution, loss of homes and assets, imprisonment and death. Pilgrims joined with the next generations, continuing GOD's plan, living in truth and peace, retaining freedom and liberty, after they were persecuted, parents put to death or imprisoned.

100 Years
1600-1700

1620 – 1732 (Georgia became a Colony)

Colonies are formed along the East Coast of America.

Founding documents for the Colonies and America were structured with the Native Indians and Pilgrims based upon Divine Law.

Pilgrims, Jews from Spain and Native Indians lived in peace.

100 Years
1700-1800

1732 (Georgia became a Colony) - 1830

The Native Indians, Jews & Pilgrims were united in their faith. They established the exact process we were to continue to follow to remain in liberty and freedom as defined within the 500 year plan to keep America united in Faith, living in Liberty and Freedom as structured within the Faith Monument pillars, exactly as the Native Indians preserved it for nearly 2200-2300 years before Europeans arrived in great numbers and changed some founding documents established for America.

The plan is clearly stated on the four pillars of the Faith Monument which was built and paid for by our Congress, dedicated in 1889, more than 100 years after we became an independent nation in 1776.

1828 Gold was discovered in Georgia and the Native Indians were forced out of their homes and off of their land due to a new law: **Native Indian Removal Act** which passed by one vote.

1830 Native Indians were 'forced out' of their homes and from their land and legally forced to proceed upon the Trail of Tears. The tears were for those who committed the crimes and atrocities, those who remained on the land GOD gave to the Native Indians.

Tears shed for the enmity Native Indians knew the 'new residents' created, trusting the 'new residents' knew not what they were 'putting into motion' between them as the new 'residents upon the land' and the Father, the Creator.

100 Years
1776-1889

1776 / 1781-3 – 1889

We focus upon July 4, 1776 as our date of becoming independent from Britain. However, GOD kept drawing my attention to 1781. Research for this date was fascinating!

1781 There was a war I was not aware of: ***Southern War Phase of the Revolutionary War.*** This war is considered to be the second half of the Revolutionary War.

The War involved Virginia, North and South Carolina, Georgia, East and West Florida. while the Revolutionary War continued as a War in the South, with the American War of Independence until September 3, 1783.

Bibles paid for by individual members of Congress, signers of the Independence with more than 50% obtaining seminary degrees.

1861 – 1865 Civil War; War Between The States.

1889 Faith Monument dedication in 1889.

100 Years
1800-1900

1804 – 1907 / 1910 / 1913

1804 Treaties for peace were arranged with the Native Indians for large parcels of land across America to operate 'in peace' while the land was taken over by new residents upon the land.

1907 President Theodore Roosevelt was 'on a hunt' while a banking crisis was declared and J P Morgan selected which banks survived the crisis; President Roosevelt retained American Government as our Republic.

1910 Federal Reserve was established, structured as an entity.

1913 President Woodrow Wilson inaugurated. Within days:

Constitutional Amendments 16 & 17 approved.

#16   Enacted Federal Reserve and the IRS.

           IRS established to collect taxes; 1st time, a Fed tax.

#17   Senators changed to popular vote status.

                 No longer 'selected' by representatives.

                 No longer able to be removed for not representing the people and replaced with those who will.

Counters our ability to remove those who do not represent us (Senators are to represent the interests of their State) and replace them with those who will represent us (from our Representatives).

Senators are to represent state interests but, they changed to represent global interests. They have also become people who are not landowners, etc., as required within the constitution so they have a 'stake' they are interested in protecting as a landowner and business owner. Political interests replaced interests of the State they represent. Within weeks and months:

Removed Ambassador to Mexico.

Re-negotiated Treaty with Mexico.

Changed American structure from Republic to Democracy.

Proceeded with an extensive 'Progressive Agenda'.

Established League of Nations; United Nations.

Involved with (credited for) Treaty of Versailles.

President Wilson given Nobel Peace Prize for the Treaty.

Leaders in the world were removed; WWI & WWII.

Actions and lies drew Americans into WWI & WWII.

(Leaders have been removed in many nations, since WWII)

146

100 Years
1830-1930

1830 – 1930

1830 American Government removed Native Indians from their homes and land.

Feds forced 17,000 from homes, marched to Oklahoma!

Gold had been discovered in Georgia in 1828, resulting in a Democrat-controlled Congress rushing through the Indian Removal Act, which passed by a single vote in 1830. It was signed by Democrat President Andrew Jackson and carried out by Democrat President Martin Van Buren.

Over 12,000 Cherokees signed a petition in protest of the Indian Removal Act. Condemning the Federal Government's mandate were members of the National Republican Party and the Whig Party, including: Rep. Abraham Lincoln, Senator Henry Clay, Senator Daniel Webster and Congressmen Davy Crockett.

The Cherokee were largely Christian and even had their own language and alphabet, created in 1821 by Cherokee silversmith Sequoyah.

Christian missionaries led resistance to the Federal Government's removal of the Indians, with many missionaries being arrested by the State of Georgia and sentenced to years of hard labor. Some were arrested for their opposition to Indian removal and their case went to the U.S. Supreme Court.

Chief Justice John Marshall ruled in favor of the Cherokee in Worcester v. Georgia (1832), writing that *the Cherokee Nation was a "distinct community" with self-government "in which the laws of Georgia can have no force."*

He (also) said, *"Thanks be to GOD, the Court can wash their hands clean of the iniquity of oppressing the Indians and disregarding their rights."*

Noting that the Supreme Court had no power to enforce its edicts, but had to rely on the President to actually implement them, Democrat President Jackson was attributed with saying: *"John Marshall has made his decision; now let him enforce it!"*

James Murray shared this summary and he credits this research to an organization established by Bill Federer, facts which are chronicled through a web site: American minute.

The Native American Indians knew the truth and 'lived in truth and peace' from about 500 BC to 1500 AD after Jews arrived from Spain and peace continued another 200 years, with the Pilgrims 100 years after 1620 and settlers arriving in the early 1700's.

Indians knew about the land, the language, the seven feasts, ten commandments, the truth about Noah/Nuah, Tower of Babel, etc.

They knew the truth about the law and GOD's plan.

1930 American Government proceeded with policies and laws resulting in:

1. Bank closures,

2. 1929 Stock Market crash,

3. Home and land foreclosures, forcing families out of their homes and off their land; Dust Bowl followed from 1930-1936.

100 Years: 1889 - 1980

1889 Faith Monument dedicated, above Plymouth Rock.

500 year plan 'carved in stone' to help until 2120.

However, Native Indians already removed 1830-1850.

1980 Georgia Guidestones, dedicated.

Coincidence?

New BRICS financial structure 2010 matches languages.

Global and ancient languages.

Eugenics and culling planned against the people.

100 Years: 1907-13 – 2007-8 / 2013

1907 - 1913 – 2007-8 / 2013

1907 America was still a Republic.

President Roosevelt repeatedly reminded Americans:

The first requisite of a good citizen in this Republic of ours is that he shall be able and willing to pull his own weight.

New York, Chamber of Commerce, 1902

The government is us; we are the government, you and I.

Asheville, North Carolina, 1902

1907 While President Theodore Roosevelt was on a hunting trip, J P Morgan Chase worked 'solo' to handle a banking crisis; arranged a program identifying which banks were solvent and which banks were not.

Quote by President Theodore Roosevelt, 1910

Our country, <u>this great republic</u>, means nothing unless it means the triumph of a real democracy, the triumph of popular government, and, in the long run, of <u>an economic system under which each man shall be guaranteed the opportunity to show the best that there is in him</u>. Osawatomie, Kansas, 1910

1910 Federal Reserve established.

1913 President Woodrow Wilson inaugurated; everything in America changed in days, weeks and months. New constitutional amendments passed by Congress within days. Federal Reserve (centralized bank), IRS. Changes nationally and globally within weeks and months.

Warning by President Thomas Jefferson:

If the American people ever allow private banks to control the issue of their currency, first by inflation, then by deflation, the banks and corporations that will grow up around the banks will

deprive the people of all property – until their children wake-up
homeless on the continent their fathers conquered.

2007-2013 Economic collapse 'layers' begin to unfold across America; mortgage industry, businesses and development industry not backed by funding in America. Business and industry closures, home owners, business owners, development industry lose homes, businesses and industries. Overnight, credit lines which were keeping businesses 'in the black' and functioning were pulled which placed the owners even further 'in debt'. Farm families of many generations are forced out of their homes and off their land due to economic collapse; only banks are bailed out, not citizens.

LORD forgive us!

LORD reveal to us everything which requires repentance so we can and our nation can restore!

LORD we will serve you in these days and stand firm in the truth and proclaim Your truth to all who have ears to hear!

LORD open the eyes of our heart, help us to see what is happening and what you are asking us to do to retain liberty and freedom, for we have believed and repeated lies, we have been proceeding as though all is well because 'me and mine are fine'.

LORD help us to see what we have not seen, so we will become people who are called by Your name and proceed by Your voice; help us stop operating as the residents of Sodom and

151

Gomorrah who became 'comfortable' in the world and did not stand firm in truth, live by faith and believe You are the only living LORD!

Thank you LORD for speaking to us in our waking and resting hours so we can hear You even when You whisper.

Thank you LORD for bringing each truth to us to repent for in these days for these are amazing days to serve You!

Thank you LORD for keeping Your hand upon us!

REVIEW   **How We Got Here, Significance to America**
                             Book Series Review

Book three in the series? Really, GOD?

Trusted everything revealed to me was already shared.

Since hindsight gives us a 20/20 view, I can finally see what readers were seeing after hearing it thousands of times: *Each book leads to the next book because of the depth to the layers, phases of the journey to the deeper truth.*

Apologies to ALL who offered deposits for the third book in the series because I trust you know by now I did not have plans for book two, let alone book three!

The new layers of lies were revealed in phases. It has helped me and I hope it is helping you to 'take it on, one phase at a time'. Trusting you are finding out the deeper truth is as shocking to me as I trust it is for you because so much was hidden from us. Over time, layers and layers of lies promoted to us as though covered up more layers of lies told to prior generations with the plan to make us believe the lies as truth and repeat it generation to generation as though it is truth.

LORD we repent for all of the lies known and unknown in these days for our desire is to hear Your voice and only listen to Your voice!

Our Father, our Yahweh, our Jehovah and our Yeshua Hamashiach, our Messiah, our Christ keep it simple: *We are either operating aligned with the Kingdom of Heaven or the other kingdom.*

Everything we say is in one kingdom or the other. We are either blessing or cursing when we speak.

Everything we do is being done in one kingdom or the other. We are either blessing or cursing when we 'do unto others'.

Bottom line:

We are either operating aligned with God's will, listening to the Holy Spirit or we are choosing to operate in our own free will and therefore, in our own power and authority. Ouch!

After years of doing all I could to 'do it all' in order to become successful in the world, I finally realized the only way to lean not on my own understanding was to lean fully on God due to being led by the Holy Spirit.

Walking slowly forward! Being led by the Holy Spirit means I do NOT know where I am being led. I'm willing to align with the will of our Father and TRUST! Finally, I reached the point where I can say to our Father 'I got it'. I've aligned with God's will to be 'spirit led' vs. following the crowd and 'doing it so I gain the approval of man'.

John 10:27. *My sheep hear My voice, and I know them, and they follow Me.*

Romans 8:14. *For as many as are led by the Spirit of God, these are sons of God.*

Acts 5:38. *And now I say to you, keep away from these men and let them alone; for if this plan or this work is of men, it will come to nothing 39 but if it is of God, you cannot overthrow it – lest you even be found to fight against God.*

Book one was released because our Father wanted us to know the truth about the condition of the church.

Scripture reference:

II Chronicles 7:14. *If My people who are called by My name will humble themselves, and pray and seek My face, and turn from their wicked ways* (REPENT), *then I will hear from heaven, and will forgive their sin and heal their land* (RESTORE).

Our stand:

1. Humble ourselves,

2. Pray & Seek GOD,

3. Turn from our wicked ways,

God's plan:

4. Hear us,

5. Forgive our sin,

6. Heal our land (our 'hunk of dust' personally)

GOD answered the cries of three internationally recognized prophets: Bob Jones, Arthur Burt and John Paul Jackson. They often traveled together and shared the pulpit together, especially in the specific churches our Father directed my path to throughout Georgia. GOD provided the word and vision to them to confirm what GOD would do for America because they cried out to know GOD's plans for His people, *For The Sake Of America.*

The prophets passed the word and vision on to people they trusted. Their people were prompted by GOD during unique experiences in my Georgia journey to provide the information to me within moments of their arrival in Macon, Georgia and following the leading of the Holy Spirit to find me:

GOD has positioned huge angelic vortexes over Macon, Georgia and Moravian Falls, North Carolina; lies / atrocities require repentance for blessings to flow again in Georgia and as believers realize the truth and repent for the atrocities, blessings will flow across America as a mighty flood.

The difference of praying through and seeking God's presence is obvious in Moravian Falls and Prayer Mountain. Trusting the work of Rick Joyner in the region is a big part of the change in the environment and atmosphere!

LORD wherever our feet are today, we take on your request of us to be led by the Holy Spirit to clearly hear what Satan does NOT want us to know about us individually, as a family and extended family so our lives, our families and our regions are healed, so the blessings will flow between us as a mighty flood until it overtakes the Eastern seaboard and expands rapidly across America as a mighty flood. We will stand firm in faith, humble ourselves, pray and seek Your truth and turn from our wicked ways so You will hear us, forgive our sin and heal our land. We will continue to praise and worship you, praying through until the path from Macon, Georgia to Moravian Falls, North Carolina is flowing with blessings and the people who witness the evidence are prompted to repent and be restored to be led by the Holy Spirit until the blessings flow in their region and overtake them, their families and region as it continues to spread across America as a mighty flood!

Book two was released for two key reasons once GOD confirmed the flow which began in Georgia exactly seven days after our President Trump was inaugurated, when he was 70 years, 7 months and 7 days old in the year of our LORD 5777 according to the Hebrew calendar. God started the flow of oil from the word.

Plus, **message direct from our Father:** We were all made in GOD's image so, WHAT WERE WE THINKING?

All divisions are NOT part of God's plan. Sectarianism is sin and fully defined in scripture.

Truth: We are all united by God and by the glory of God, as Jesus clearly defined within **John 17:22.** *And the glory which You gave Me I have given them, that they may be one just as We are one.* God's plan is for us to be one as Christ and our Father are one! So, as God repeated a few times, WHAT WERE WE THINKING?

1. We are all created in GOD's image and yet, some groups think they have rights other groups do not have and 'in the process' we enslaved, auctioned, lynched and killed GOD's chosen people,

Scripture reference:

Genesis 1:27. *So <u>God created man in His own image; in the image of God He created him; male and female He created them.</u>*

This scripture reference also confirmed GOD created both in His own image and Hebrew words for our Father and our Christ are male with a female word for Holy Spirit.

2. We focused upon becoming successful in the world, proceeding as the world proceeds vs. seeking and listening to the only true voice to follow the truth, the word, our LORD & SAVIOR, and our FATHER. **Concluding statement:** *Will Jesus recognize us as 'My people' or will He say He never knew us?*

Scripture reference:

John 10:27. *My sheep hear My voice, and I know them, and they follow Me.*

After the second book was released, so many people confirmed they were shocked to realize how critical it is to:

1. Hear the voice of the LORD,

2. Discern the voice of the LORD,

3. ONLY proceed & act upon promptings of GOD and CHRIST per the voice of the LORD confirmed to us by the Holy Spirit.

As believers, this is how we are to operate each day.

Do we take a meeting we are asked to take if GOD is not prompting us to take the meeting?

Do we decline the meeting when GOD prompts?

Is GOD revealing a word for someone when they cross our path? Do we take the time to deliver the word, GOD's message?

Do we listen so we clearly know before we leave our home what we are to take with us when we leave the house so we will not proceed 'in lack' during our journey?

GOD confirmed everything for the suitcase, every time He arranged the 'next assignment'.

GOD prompted me to take things which I questioned at the time. However, He knows the weather, the seasons in the Southern Hemisphere are opposite to the seasons in the Northern Hemisphere and He knows what we do not know before we leave home and before we accept or arrive 'on assignment', before we are aware we are going to meet with people or deliver a word.

In ALL things, GOD prepares us prior to each step so we will be ready 'in the day' when we need to be ready.

I Corinthians 2:14. *But the natural man does not receive the things of the Spirit of God, for they are foolishness to him; nor can he know them, because they are spiritually discerned.*

GOD guides us 'on purpose' when we are willing to 'be trained'.

Often when I respond, *"I'm in training"* people are shocked, especially the people who are around me more often since they have heard me say it once or twice before (or more often) because the world wants us to 'already be fully trained' to be 'trained up to be successful within the world plan' before we proceed.

It's different with GOD since He is 'ever present' and He guides us moment by moment, 24/7.

GOD wants us to remain flexible, teachable, trainable so we will serve as true representatives, ambassadors for Christ.

Even pastors and ministry leaders were asking me how it would be possible to only proceed according to the voice and promptings of the LORD. They focused upon becoming bible scholars.

MORE PRAYER, REPENTANCE and RESTORATION of believers, pastors and ministry leaders. Powerful assignments!

Honored to be one believer who GOD can use to change a life, a ministry, a church, a region or a nation.

Grateful to be available to touch hearts and see lives change for the glory of GOD!

Christ confirmed to our Father in **John 17:22.** *And the glory which You gave Me I have given them, that they may be one just as We are one.*

We have everything required to do all GOD asks of us!

Just when I trusted it was finally time for me to proceed toward the publishing dates for the four books and a special devotional which were set aside to structure *For The Sake Of America* and *For The Sake Of America II,* GOD revealed more and more and more facts which were not included in the second book.

Full days and nights. Lots of research regarding the lies so the real facts, the truth can be revealed. Intense hours! The enemy has influenced so much across America! Praying we will join together 'in GOD's plan, His glory, united as 'one' seeking His truth' in these days!

It's exciting to proceed with our Father and gain His view of the extensive effort undertaken by our defeated enemy which attempts, daily, to direct us away from our Father's plan for our life and our nation.

Wow! GOD loves us so much He sent His ONLY son for each of us to learn the truth: Christ is the ONLY way, the word & truth!

Book three. Today, since we are embarking together into the third phase of seeking the deeper truth, uncovering more layers; lies used to hide the truth from us, our Father prompted me to share two specific scriptures 'in context' because we only hear the verses:

161

John 10:27. *My sheep hear My voice, and I know them, and they follow Me.*

Romans 8:14. *For as many as are led by the Spirit of God, these are sons of God.*

For the truth is the truth!

Acts 5:38. *And now I say to you, keep away from these men and let them alone; for if this plan or this work is of men, it will come to nothing* **39** *but if it is of God, you cannot overthrow it – lest you even be found to fight against God.*

Verses gain a deeper meaning when viewed 'in context'.

Christ confirmed in John 10:22-30.

The Shepherd Knows His Sheep

Now it was the Feast of Dedication in Jerusalem, and it was winter.

23 And Jesus walked in the temple, in Solomon's porch.

24 Then the Jews surrounded Him and said to Him, *"How long do You keep us in doubt? If You are the Christ, tell us plainly."*

25 Jesus answered them, *"I told you, and you do not believe. The works that I do in My Father's name, they bear witness of Me.*

26 *But you do not believe, because you are not of My sheep, as I said to you.*

27 <u>*My sheep hear My voice, and I know them, and they follow Me.*</u>

28 *And I give them eternal life, and they shall never perish; neither shall anyone snatch them out of My hand.*

29 *My Father, who has given them to Me, is greater than all; and no one is able to snatch them out of My Father's hand.*

30 *I and My Father are one."*

Romans 8:12-17.

Sonship Through the Spirit

Therefore, brethren, we are debtors – not to the flesh, to live according to the flesh. **13** *For if you live according to the flesh you will die; but if by the Spirit you put to death the deeds of the body, you will live.*

14 <u>*For as many as are led by the Spirit of God, these are sons of God.*</u>

15 *For you did not receive the spirit of bondage again to fear, but you received the Spirit of adoption by whom we cry out, "Abba, Father."*

16 *The Spirit Himself bears witness with our spirit that we are children of God,* **17** *and if children, then heirs – heirs of God and joint heirs with Christ, if indeed we suffer with Him, that we may also be glorified together.*

Choose:

Only two choices, options which have not changed in centuries:

1. Choose Baal (other gods), or

2. Choose the only living Lord.

The roots in Georgia, the problems in America are based upon the exact same choices!

Choose this day whom you will serve.

All rights and freedoms were available to the believers of the only living LORD.

We did not retain the freedoms we were given.

Now, we are at a critical point of losing rights and freedoms.

No matter what we are facing, the choice is the same!

Choose this day who you will serve:

1. Choose Baal (other gods), or

2. Choose the only living Lord.

John 10:27. *My sheep hear My voice, and I know them, and they follow Me.*

Romans 8:14. *For as many as are led by the Spirit of God, these are sons of God.*

LORD we repent for everything, all that we thought was truth and all that we did not realize was a lie. Speak to us in our waking and resting hours. May we hear only Your voice even when you whisper! Open the eyes of our heart.

In the mighty and matchless name of our LORD and SAVIOR Jesus Christ, our Yeshua Hamashiach we pray!

AMEN (our GOD is a faithful King!)

Research

1.   Baldwin, Georgia City web site.

2.   End Times Prophecy Alerts Blogspot RE: Cherokee Nation Ancient Hebrew Tribe.

3.   Georgia Encyclopedia. James Oglethorpe established structure of the Colony of Georgia in 1732 for Britain; led expedition of colonists to settle on Georgia land in 1733.

4.   Hillah, ancient city in Iraq, Capitol of Babylon; first city Marines were ordered to protect during war in Iraq.

5.   Obituary of Robert Clark Cook

6.   Biography of Margaret Sanger (1879-1966)

7.   Biography of Madame Helena Petrovna Blavatsky, born nee Princess Hahn in 1831.

8.   Biography of Alice (Evans) Bailey and Foster Bailey.

9.   Biography of Alice and Walter Evan's daughters (later each daughter added the name of Bailey): Dorothy, Mildred & Ellison; son of Ellison and Arthur Gordon Poynter Leahy and one son Arthur Ronald William Leahy, born in Pakistan in 1944.

10.   LDS Women of God, Chabad and Pealim web sites for Hebrew meaning of words.

11.   Letters provided by member of Philomathea # 25 in Elberton, Georgia, shortly before his death to blog of Van's Hardware and Farm Supply.

1. Prayer of Release for Freemasons and Their Descendants

Available to read direct from web sites.

I've researched a few web sites and Restoration in Christ Ministries is the version which is the closest one to the version I've used within many prayer sessions the past few years.

1. Be sure to include at least two witnesses! Helpful to have family members attend the prayer session, if possible.

2. Be sure to stop after each paragraph! Make sure everyone is OK and they are not experiencing a physical reaction to the information. Also, be sure to ask if anything came to mind during the reading of each paragraph.

The testimonies are amazing! I could fill another book!

Example: One of the special experiences shared during the reading of the prayer with two children in their 60's and their father in his 80's who proceeded through the Masonic oath process through each degree to the 32nd degree.

His family was not aware of the fact he was threatened by many members that he had to take the oath for the 33rd degree or the members would kill him, burn down his business and his home.

He was concerned so he shared the threat with his pastor. At the time, his pastor led him through a very brief three-page prayer to renounce the oaths taken. He was not aware of the fact his pastor was also a member of the same Masonic Lodge. His pastor was sworn to secrecy, exactly as each member taking the oaths. If members of the Lodge are asked anything about the members of the Masonic Lodge or the oaths and activities, members are sworn to secrecy and they are required to deny the truth.

His pastor met with the leadership of the Masonic Lodge and confirmed he would not be a problem to the Lodge in the future.

When we met to pray, he laughed because he is still alive and all of the men who threatened him are dead and buried in the local cemetery.

Plus, we reached a point during the renouncing of the oaths when a very long name was the focus of the oath. His daughter said she knew the name. He was shocked to hear this because He never shared anything about the Masonic oaths with anyone in his family.

His daughter said it happened when she was eight. Her friend received a Ouija board and she wanted one. While 'playing' she said she told her friend she was going to leave her hands off the planchette (movable piece used on the Ouija board) to see what it would do if she was not touching it. The planchette moved letter to letter and pointed to a series of letters which became the same spelling of the long name within the oath.

NOTE: I had to look up planchette because it was a new term to me. A planchette is the small, heart-shaped board supported by casters, fitted with a vertical pencil used for automatic writing and in seances. Wow! How many families knew this truth?

When she shared that she was eight at the time, her father realized he was taking the oath to that name at the time she was eight years old.

Prayers are with you that you and your family shall become free from any hold by the enemy for any reason!

2. The Father's Blessing*

So many blessings begin to flow within a person, their family and extended family once they are validated through The Father's Blessing. Typically, we link our relationship with our Heavenly Father to the type of relationship we have or had with our earthly father.

Then, we spend our lifetime limiting GOD!

Proceed with two people involved. One person to pray through with you and one person to read the blessing and give you a validation hug.

The release of 'stuff' during each forgiveness confession is significant each time the blessing is spoken over the life of a willing participant. The freedom felt when the validation hug is provided at the conclusion results in amazing testimonies!

First:

Ask forgiveness for what you have done. The following is a suggested list that might be helpful. Also ask them, "What else?" It is important to know what is in their memories.

Please forgive me:

...for not protecting you and making you feel safe

...for not showing you respect for your uniqueness and not giving you the freedom to form your own opinions and express them

...for not being the boy/girl I wanted

...for not living up to my expectations

...for not being at your sports games, for not giving you my time and attention

...for not remembering birthdays and other special days

...for not providing for you financially, for not being dependable or trustworthy

...for not apologizing to you and admitting when I was wrong

...for not having integrity and keeping my word

...for not keeping my promises to you

...for my temper and anger, for teaching or correcting you without judgment or control

...for not being a proper, godly example, for being religious, keeping you under the law, so that I would look good

...for not telling you "I love you" and hugging you regularly

...for the word curses spoken to you (i.e., you are stupid, lazy, no good, sissy, etc.)

...for not loving your mother, for the physical or emotional abuse of her

...for not meeting your mother's needs, for being selfish and manipulative

...for not spending time with you and the family

...for not establishing what a father/husband is and their responsibility

...for divorcing your mom and abandoning you

...for abandoning you emotionally and physically

...for not teaching you how to relate to men (daughter)

...for my silence toward you

...for not teaching you how to relate to women (son), for not teaching you to be emotionally intimate

...for not building you up and encouraging you, for not believing in you

...for not teaching you to be responsible by facing consequences that result from disobedience

...for showing favoritism among the kids

...for yelling at you and for cursing you

...for embarrassing you in front of others

...for not validating your femininity as a daughter

...for not validating your masculinity as a son

...for not being a godly father, for not praying for you

...for not teaching you about God

...for not teaching you about life skills

...for not recognizing the gifts God has given you

...for not teaching you godly sexuality

...for not modeling God in your life or establishing a healthy picture of God

…for not practicing unconditional love

…for conceiving you out of wedlock

…for not setting boundaries and not teaching you how to say 'no'

…for expecting you to act like an adult and not allowing you to enjoy your childhood

…for not taking a stand for what is right and setting limits, etc.

Have I hurt you in any other way?

Second:

In the name of Jesus, I command all the spirits of fear, rejection, and abandonment that came to you in my sins to go now.

Third:

I bless you my precious child. You are so loved, specially created by God, unique and perfect. I am so proud of you. I honor you. I speak life to every cell in your body. You are the son/daughter God delights in and I have the special privilege to call you my child and to watch you mature. I am proud of you, I speak life into you.

I bless you with God's richest blessings for your life. May you be filled with the new wine and prosper as your soul prospers.

I bless that you may be filled with God's desire and grace so that you may please God in all that you are and all that you do, so you can be that child God intended you to be.

I bless you with the blessing of Ephraim and Manasseh that you will forget the pain of your past and that your future will be fruitful.

Fourth:

I command the diseases (name them) to go in the name of Jesus.

174

3. The Mother's Blessing*

First:

Ask forgiveness for what you have done. The following is a suggested list that might be helpful. Also ask them, "what else?" It is important to know what is in their memories.

Please forgive me for not wanting you, for not bonding with you in the womb. Forgive me for conceiving you out of wedlock. It is not your fault-you were not a mistake. Will you forgive me?

I did not hold you to my breast and speak to you and give you the love you needed for security. Will you forgive me?

Forgive me for being so critical of you, for yelling at you, for saying things that devalued you, for not telling you how very valuable you are. Will you forgive me?

I did not nurture you, or comfort you or hold you when you hurt. Will you forgive me for abandoning you emotionally and physically?

Forgive me for not taking time to meet your needs or to spend tie with you. Will you forgive me?

I didn't let you enjoy just being a child. I talked to you about things you were not mature enough to deal with that made you afraid. Please forgive me for stealing your childhood by not letting you express yourself, for expecting you to take on my responsibilities. Will you forgive me?

You felt you had to perform for my love because I did not show you unconditional love. Will you forgive me?

I did not protect you from all the fussing and fighting in the home. Will you forgive me?

Please forgive me for not stopping the inappropriate spankings or abuse-verbal, physical, or sexual, for not believing you and not protecting you-for not telling you that it was not your fault. It's not your fault.

175

Forgive me for all the ways I was unapproachable or did not listen when you needed to talk to me. Will you forgive me?

I was not there when you came home and you were lonely. I was not there when you were afraid. I did not protect you from bullies. Will you forgive me?

I was controlling to get you to do things my way. Forgive me for controlling your every action and for setting myself up as a god in your life. I always had to be right. Will you forgive me?

Forgive me for not modeling what a Godly wife and mother should be, for not being vulnerable to you.

Forgive me for not teaching you how to be emotionally intimate, to set appropriate boundaries, for not teaching you how to relate to men or women.

I ask for your forgiveness for all the ways I fell short of nurturing you and not being there for you when you needed me. I was wrong and I'm sorry.

Have I hurt you in any other way?

Second:

In the name of Jesus, I command all the spirits of fear, rejection, and abandonment that came to you in my sins to go now.

Third:

I bless you my precious child. You are so loved, specially created by God, unique and perfect. I am so proud of you. I honor you. I speak life to every cell in your body. You are the son/daughter God delights in and I have the special privilege to call you my child and to watch you mature. I am proud of you, I speak life into you.

I bless you with God's richest blessings for your life. May you be filled with new wine and prosper as your soul prospers.

I bless that you may be filled with God's desires and grace so that you may please God in all that you are and all that you do, so you can be that child God intended you to be.

I bless you my precious child, you are so loved, specially created by God, unique and perfect. I am so proud of you.

I bless the work of your hands, your gifts and abilities.

I bless your heart to know love and give love. To know God intimately, love Him intimately and serve Him.

I bless your emotions, your relationships with God, your spouse and others.

I bless you that you may be a Godly role model and witness to others.

I bless your heart that your spouse and friends can safely trust in it, that you will have a grateful heart and be thankful for all you have been given.

I bless your provision for your family in food, clothing, love, warmth, and understanding.

I bless your watchful eye over your household to provide for your family and not eat the bread of idleness and share what you have with others.

I bless your fear of the Lord, to follow His commandments and desire to have order and balance in your life.

I bless you and your wisdom and strength that comes from God, and I respect and honor your spouse and your family.

I bless you to prosper and be in health, even as your soul prospers.

You are fearfully and wonderfully made and I bless you. I am so very proud of you.

I give you life as your mother; I speak life to every cell of your body. I release you and give you permission to be the man or woman God intended you to be.

Before you were born God loved you and I love you. I honor you, I praise God for you, I bless you now and forever.

I bless you with the blessing of Ephraim and Manasseh, that you will forget the pain of your past and that your future will be fruitful.

Fourth:

I command the diseases (name them) to go in the name of Jesus.

*Harvest Time International Ministries takes no credit for writing this prayer. We obtained this prayer through Wellspring Ministries of Anchorage, Alaska.

Feel free to check out their website: akwellspring.com

A Personal Note Just Between Us

Hope For Believers

Hope For America

LORD thank You for Your promise! Thank You for providing the angelic vortexes over Macon, Georgia and Moravian Falls, North Carolina 'For The Sake Of America'!

Grateful to know Your hand is upon us and You will never leave us or forsake us! Thank You for providing Your truth in Your word and through Your prophets so we will be prepared to march with You before the SONrise!

For I was humbled when You shared the word with me to share to a special leader in the body of Christ after You provided the same vision of the 'war room', including the same furniture:

"Not enough of my men are preparing and putting on their steel toed boots to march with Me, so I am having to call forth My women, even My widows and My orphans, to prepare My Army to march with Me before the SONrise."

Forgive us LORD for all of the lies shared, all of our misunderstandings passed on generation to generation!

We truly want You to recognize us as Your people who are called by Your name!

Amen (Hebrew meaning, Our GOD is a Faithful KING!)

To live from glory to glory, it is important to comprehend that our Savior, Jesus Christ, the Messiah, as confirmed in **John 17:22**, gave us the glory that we would be one, united together 'In One Accord' as He and the Father are one. He gave us this truth, while He was with us! Blessings upon you until the next ONE MORE TIME* our LORD brings us together!

Sheila

Email: hisbest4usorders@gmail.com

Ephesians 2:19-22 *We are no longer foreigners and aliens, but fellow citizens...*
II Corinthians 12:14-15. (a) *"Now, I am ready to visit you...*
II Corinthians 13:11-14. *Aim for perfection ...*

* While in Ghana, West Africa for the coronation of a King, Bishop Duncan William's worship team sang a simple verse: ONE MORE TIME, ONE MORE TIME, HE HAS ALLOWED US TO COME TOGETHER ONE MORE TIME, and by the third time they shared this verse, pointing to each other, then, to each of us on the platform and then, to each of the participants speaking at least 13 Afrikaans dialects and nine foreign languages, there was not a dry eye in the house!

Books Authored by Sheila Holm

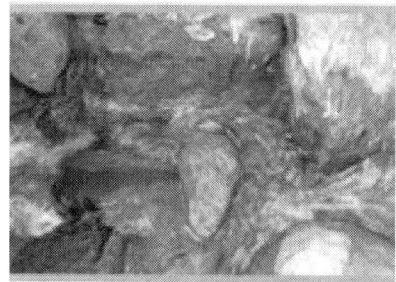

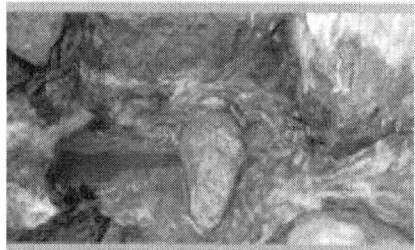

A WAKE UP CALL: IT'S RESTORATION TIME!

MYSTERIES REVEALED: HOW AND WHEN THE CHURCH WAS DECEIVED AND WHAT IS REQUIRED FOR FULL RESTORATION.

SHEILA HOLM

IN SEARCH OF WIGGLESWORTH

A JOURNEY WHICH SPEAKS TO THE VERY CORE OF WHAT IT MEANS TO BE A TRUE BROTHER AND SISTER IN CHRIST!

SHEILA HOLM

In One Accord

One body, one Spirit, one hope, one Lord, one faith, one baptism;, one God & Father of all, who is above all & through all, and in you all. Ephesians 4:4-6

Sheila Holm

A PECULIAR PEOPLE

A holy nation, a peculiar people.

We are not ashamed of the Gospel of Jesus Christ!!

DISCIPLESHIP OF PECULIAR PEOPLE BY PECULIAR PEOPLE

SHEILA HOLM

ALWAYS SPEAK LIFE

FOR THE EYES OF THE LORD ARE ON THE
RIGHTEOUS, AND HIS EARS ARE OPEN
TO THEIR PRAYERS ... 1 PETER 3:12

SHEILA HOLM

CHRISTMAS

MYSTERIES UNCOVERED & REVEALED:
TRUTH REGARDING THE BIRTH OF
THE MESSIAH, HIDDEN SINCE 300 AD

SHEILA HOLM

FOR THE SAKE OF AMERICA

AMERICA IS IN TROUBLE
THE ROOT PROBLEMS AND THE
PROMISES OF THE LORD ARE REVEALED
FOR THE SAKE OF AMERICA!

SHEILA HOLM

FOR THE SAKE OF AMERICA II

ANCIENT AND CURRENT ROOTS REVEALED
REPENTANCE FOR DEEPER TRUTH REQUIRED
THEN, THE LORD'S BLESSINGS WILL FLOW AS A
RESTORATION FLOOD FOR THE SAKE OF AMERICA!

SHEILA HOLM

Releasing soon

CHOOSING THE 12

WHO INFLUENCE CHOICE

SHEILA HOLM

ALIGN

WITH THE KINGDOM OF HEAVEN

SHEILA HOLM

My Story in HIStory
Sheila Holm

Nation Restoration

Published in 2014

Seven Step Business Plan

Published, 2007

Latin America edition:

Spanish Language

Published, 2009

ACKNOWLEDGMENTS

AFRICA

Ghana, West Africa

Pastor Sam,

"Truly, GOD has sent you to us with a strong word for our church."

Pastor Charles,

"It blesses my soul to hear of your faith & see the fruit of the ministry."

Johannesburg, South Africa

Pastor Jhanni,

"GOD is doing a good work through you and I pray with you and our church."

Coronation Ceremony

AMERICA

Bishop George Dallas McKinney, California

"Sheila is GOD's ambassador to encourage Christians, especially pastors, throughout the US, Africa, Australia and Europe. Without sponsors or any visible means of support, she has traveled the world sustained by the faithfulness of GOD.

Dr. Nancy Franklin, Georgia

"Thank you God for answering my prayers by sending Your apostle to (the region) to unite the believers ... "

Prophetess Nancy Haney, Alaska

"God has never given me this before. I see circles and circles and circles ... you drink and you draw from one circle to the other, and that's what you do, you drink and draw and you bring these circles together ... Pulling many groups together. All these groups need each other ... He can use you for you have ears to hear and you hear His deep truth. You are filtering what is nonsense and what is real ... because you have been in that circle, and because of what you say they are going to merge. It is going to expand, become bigger than you could imagine."

Pastor, Host of "Praise the Lord", TBN,

"...The fruit of the ministry is evident in your testimony..."

Man of God (Georgia), Requesting to be Discipled while attending the coronation of a King in Africa, Georgia

"...at my age, it is hard to believe I am learning so much in these few days about what I did not know...realizing what it is to know that I know how it is to live within God's word each day. Will you consider discipling me?"

International Prophet,

"You have remained steadfast to God's plan and God will continue to send you forth for His plan and purpose to be fulfilled, and for the thousands who have not knelt..."

President, Christian Publishing Company

"Only God could orchestrate such a grand plan..."

Prayer Director, International Prayer Center

"God is opening many doors for you..."

Christian Publisher, "God has given you a powerful voice and a sweet spirit..."

Pastor, Southern California

"God is raising you up and sending you forth to many nations..."

International Apostle

"God is doing a mighty work through you, for His righteousness precedes you, showers over you and follows you as a mighty wake. May it continue for each of your days…"

Prophetic Prayer Partner, Minnesota

"Only God could walk you through these days… accomplish so much through you, in the midst of your daily situations, the many blessings shared during each of your travels will continue to shower blessings upon each of the many households around the world…"

AUSTRALIA

Four Square Gospel Church, Aboriginal Cultural Center

Pastor Rex, "**GOD blessed us through your preaching on Easter Sunday. We will never forget that you were in our midst … GOD brought new people to Jesus today and we thank GOD for what He has done because you answered His call.**"

Newcastle, New South Wales, Australia

Pastor Mark, "**…the staff and business leaders heard the message of Personal and Professional Life Management this week, so we are blessed you agreed to preach the word to our church this morning.**"

Prayer Team Meeting "**We know now how we will we be able to continue this mighty work when you are not in our midst…**"

ENGLAND

London, England

Pastor Vincent, Glory House, East London, "*…the honor is ours this Easter Sunday.*"

Associate Pastor, "*The Glory of our GOD Almighty shines upon you and through you in your speaking and your actions…we give Him praise.*"

Protocol Team,

"**GOD has mightily blessed us by sending you into our midst.**"

Pastor Arnold,

"***You have blessed the people of this congregation, and in His wisdom and timing, may He bring you back into our midst again, very soon.***"

Pastor, West London,

"**We rejoice with you in hearing and   seeing   the mighty things GOD is doing.**"

Pastor, South London, **"Our GOD is evidenced in your life and your speaking, while we continue to thank GOD for the work He is doing through you..."**

High Commissioner, Kingdom of Tonga, serving in the Embassy in London, England; Ambassador Akosita, **"GOD's timing is always right...for you to be with us, prior to the Economic Summit, to meet and pray with us..."**

Sunderland, England

Anglican, Former Church of Pastor Smith Wigglesworth

Pastor Day, **"I thank GOD for sending you to our church this morning, for serving communion to me, and for renewing and restoring me for the call upon my life."**

Kingdom of TONGA

Pastor Isileli Taukolo, "**Our board and business leaders were fasting and praying and GOD confirmed He was sending someone to us. We are deeply touched by the message GOD sent to us, through you.**"

Minister of Finance, Tasi, "**Our meeting was an answer to my prayers, and I thank you for providing the seminar for our senior staff members, and meeting with them individually for prayer and coaching.**"

Government Office, "**Thank you for speaking today and for staying and praying with us.**"

Interpreter, Sela

About the Author

The LORD fulfills upon His promises within the scriptures. He has equipped and trained Sheila while He:

- Places her feet on the soil of each continent,

- Sends her forth without an extra coin or tunic,

- Arranges flights and accommodations in each nation,

- Introduces her before she arrives,

- Lifts her up and encourages her,

- Seats her before governors and kings,

- Fills her as an empty vessel,

- Shares His wisdom and word of knowledge,

- Blesses and heals the people in her path,

- Comforts & re-encourages her to encourage pastors, prophets, apostles, believers, teachers & evangelists,

- Touches people individually in conferences/multitude,
- Speaks through her with power and authority,
- Takes people into gift of laughter when she preaches,
- Addresses situations the body of Christ is facing,
- Unites the people in the region,
- Confirms His word through her with each prayer & message shared,
- Speaks through her so people hear His words in their own language, especially when the translators also experience the gift of laughter and stop translating,
- Directs her path to <u>speak life</u> into each situation whether GOD sends people to her to be re-encouraged or he asks her to pray with a pastor, the church, or someone in a store or a restaurant, etc.

Vision and word **For The Sake Of America** were given to internationally recognized prophets. They were not able to be 'boots on ground' in Georgia so they shared the facts with people they trusted. Then, the vision and word were released to Sheila because she agreed to remain and fulfill upon the assignment after she traveled across country to Georgia for three specific weeks in October 2013. The third message from the man who received the vision and word from Bob Jones activated Sheila to proceed with the research.

Sheila was not aware of the LORD's plan to extend her time from three weeks to three years or that He would reveal such deep truth to her *For the Sake of America!*

She did not realize the LORD would extend her in Georgia for another year while the 'deeper truth' of the ancient and current roots were being revealed to her, one layer at a time. However, the LORD confirmed in a specific vision that He sent her to Georgia because she asked for the assignment.

Since Georgia was not part of her conversations with the LORD she was a bit surprised until the LORD reminded her of her own words each time she witnessed the flow of the body of Christ in other nations He sent her to around the world. She hoped the LORD would send someone to bring the truth to the body of Christ in America.

When the LORD reminded her of her heart's desire, she realized in that moment He sent her to Georgia to be available during this critical time in our nation for His purpose, plan and promise to be made known to the people.

The LORD promised once the Ancient and Current Roots Are Revealed, Repentance of the Deeper Truth is Required. Then, the LORD's Blessings Will Flow As A Restoration Flood *For The Sake Of America!*

She trusted GOD's promise was fulfilled upon. The LORD has continued to provide 'deeper truth' in *For The Sake Of America II* more deeper truth was revealed to her, resulting in *For The Sake Of America III*.

GOD has taken Sheila around the world, church to church, business to business, nation to nation, set her before governors and kings without an extra coin or tunic.

Many confirm she walks in the five-fold ministry. She does not use a title because GOD does the work while He sends her as an apostle and prophet, and He orchestrates all arrangements for her to preach, teach, and evangelize.

People attending the conferences often say her segments are like watching someone walk out of the bible, share for a while and then, go right back in the bible, aka continue upon her journey in HIStory.

26885553R00113

Made in the USA
San Bernardino, CA
22 February 2019